Y0-AGJ-885

# AMERICA'S WAR ON DRUGS

# AMERICA'S WAR ON DRUGS

## BY JOAN J. JOHNSON

*Franklin Watts/New York/London/Toronto/Sydney/1990*

Photographs courtesy of: Gamma-Liaison: pp. 11 (Arnaud Borrell), 22, 64, 148 (all Stephen Ferry), 69 (Max Pages), 76 (G. Noel-Figaro), 127 (Jean Marc Giboux); Picture Group: pp. 14 (Steve Starr), 98 (Danford Connely); Photo Researchers: pp. 38 (Ulrike Welsch), 100 (James Prince); Impact Visuals: p. 42 (Joe Fish); Reuters/Bettmann Newsphotos: p. 46; Magnum Photos: pp. 54 (F. Scianna), 74 (Abbas), 82 (Alex Webb), 108 (Eugene Richards); UPI/Bettmann Newsphotos: pp. 88, 141; Black Star: p. 118 (Tom Sobolik).

Library of Congress Cataloging-in-Publication Data

Johnson, Joan (Joan J.)
    America's war on drugs / Joan J. Johnson.
        p.     cm.
    Includes bibliographical references.
    Summary: Examines American efforts to thwart the attempts of drug suppliers to smuggle illegal substances into the country.
    ISBN 0-531-15179-4   ISBN 0-531-10954-2 (lib. bdg.)
    1. Narcotics, Control of—United States—Juvenile literature.
    [1. Narcotics, Control of.   2. Drug traffic.]   I. Title.
    HV5825.J623   1990
    363.4'5'0973—dc20                                        90-32994
                                                                  CIP
                                                                  AC

 **CONTENTS**

# AMERICA'S WAR ON DRUGS

# 1
# THE
# DRUG EPIDEMIC

Imagine, if you can, a world in which no addictive drugs existed. Imagine a world in which drugs had never existed, in which no problems stemming from drug abuse had ever occurred. How many crimes—thefts, bribes, murders and rapes, terrorist bombings and gangland executions—might never have been committed? How many famous people—actors, rock stars, athletes—would still be alive? How many people you know would not be talking about drugs, experimenting with drugs, or buying, selling, or abusing drugs?

So widespread is the abuse of drugs in the United States that anyone old enough to read this book has been touched in some way by the drug culture. The lucky may only know of a celebrity who overdosed or a movie about drug abuse or a song with references to drugs. For many people, however, a world without addictive drugs would require erasing whole blocks of their own personal experience: people they've known; events they've attended; conversations they've had; minutes, hours, days, months and even years of their lives. For an increasing number of people, drugs are creating memories they will never forget.

- In a Detroit hospital, a 3-pound (about 1.5-kg) newborn flails its fists back and forth in the jerky, cranky manner typical of crack babies. Because his mother is an addict, he will suffer severe diarrhea, fail to feed properly, and need twice-a-day doses of laudanum, a solution of opium, alcohol, and water, to keep him sedated. If he survives, his mother wants to keep him. At least, that is what she said when she was discharged more than a week ago. She has not visited her baby since.

- In Westchester County, New York, the number of children neglected or abused by their parents has tripled in ten years. Social service agencies attribute the increase to drug abuse. Nationwide, grandmothers and other older relatives living in drug-ravaged inner-cities now raise seven out of every ten children because their mothers are crack addicts. Experts say that never has a drug been so totally incapacitating or so popular among women.

- In Philadelphia, psychologist Dr. Anna Childress describes the destruction crack can wreak on the lives of those who merely experiment with it. She tells reporter Pamela Zurer about a middle-aged patient whose life was destroyed within two years after trying crack. The man held a steady job for sixteen years, had a good marriage, had no trouble controlling his alcohol use, and had never been tempted to try other drugs. For his fortieth birthday, a friend persuaded him to try crack. That was the turning point in his life. Since then, he has hocked his possessions and lost both his job and his family. Dr. Childress says, "I would have been hard put to predict this guy would have had trouble with an addictive problem. That was before crack cocaine."

Crack's effect on young addicts is equally startling. In Detroit, a Little League team folded one recent spring for lack of enough players. Selling crack had replaced playing baseball. At night in Houston, teenage dealers supporting their own habits flick cigarette lighters to attract drivers looking for a drug buy. The

Crack is a smokable, extremely addictive
form of cocaine. Some have called it the
"fast food of drugs" because it is sold
in small quantities and gives the user
a quick, but temporary, high.

neighborhood has deteriorated so much that legitimate businesses are going broke for lack of customers. On the streets of our cities, teenage prostitutes sell their bodies, often for as little as the $10 they need for a fix.

Drug dealers have become so brazen that they don't even seem to fear the law. Teenage gang assassinations over drug-selling turf take place at midday on the busiest street corners. "You don't kill no mother from across the street," *Atlantic Monthly* reporter Gustavo Gorriti quoted one young hit man as saying. "You walk up to him, you kill him in his head." In February 1988, three young men walked up to the car of New York City police officer Edward Byrne and executed him as he sat inside. In Washington, D.C., drug-related street crime has increased so much that President George Bush and his drug-policy adviser, William Bennett, have considered using federal troops to control the situation.

But street crime isn't the only thing taxing law enforcement agencies and the United States judicial system. In February 1989, Attorney General Dick Thornburgh announced the arrest of thirty-three "respectable" people who represented equally "respectable" corporations for laundering $500 million, and possibly as much as $1 billion, in cocaine profits through jewelry merchants from Los Angeles to Florida over a period of two years.

Law enforcement officials are only too aware that $500 million is just the tip of the iceberg of drug profits being illegally hidden by supposedly first-rate citizens. Customs officials on Cyprus, an island in the Mediterranean Sea, say they have seen in one day as much as $50 million pass through their country on its way to Switzerland, where access to the identity of depositors and the amount of their bank accounts is not easily obtainable. Estimates of the profits of the Colombian drug traffickers alone are as high as $4 billion per year.

In the United States, people are afraid for good reason. It is true that drugs have always existed. The United States has always had smugglers and processors, pushers and addicts to contend with. It has even had other drug scares—one back in the early 1900s and another in the 1960s. Yet never has the world of drug crime and drug addiction posed such a danger to society, and that danger is increasing.

While recent statistics show that the use of most illegal drugs—heroin, marijuana, and synthetic drugs such as PCP and LSD—has leveled off and that the casual use of these drugs has decreased, the use of crack, a smokable, extremely addictive form of cocaine, is on the increase. This is especially true among the young and the poor, for whom the drug was created.

The origin of the term "crack" is unclear. Some believe it is named for the crackling sound it makes when smoked. Others attribute the name to the drug's resemblance to cracked paint chips or plaster. Crack is cheap, readily available, easy to use, and difficult to detect. This adds up to an extremely attractive package for large segments of the population. According to the Rand Corporation, 4.8 percent of all high school seniors in 1988 had tried crack. Another 14 percent said they had used cocaine in other forms. Among slightly older men and women, college students and others in their early twenties, 40 percent had tried cocaine. All told, figures from the National Institute on Drug Abuse (NIDA) estimate an astounding 35 to 40 million Americans have tried cocaine. Additional data compiled from drug abuse hotlines, emergency rooms, and police arrest files indicate that a growing proportion are smoking crack.

### Antidrug Tactics

While crack use increases, those fighting the war on drugs are unsure about the most effective way to stop drugs. Americans, from average citizens to top government officials involved in developing and carrying out antidrug policies, hold a confusing number of often contradictory opinions on how to win the war on drugs. But all proposed methods of stanching the flow of drugs fall into two major categories: "demand-side" and "supply-side" tactics.

*A close-up of crack and crack vials.*

Demand-side tactics are aimed at the consumers of drugs, the millions of Americans who support the illegal drug industry by purchasing anything from an occasional marijuana joint to a steady supply of injectable heroin. The goal of demand-side tactics is drying up the market for drugs so that the drug trafficking industry will wither and die from lack of profit. Demand-side tactics include rehabilitation of addicts, who are the source of the illegal drug industry's profits, and preventive education, especially of young people, the group that is the drug industry's new sales target. Other demand-side tactics include stricter penalties for users, drug testing, and changing the image of drugs so that people not only wouldn't dare to use them but wouldn't even want to try.

Supply-side tactics, on the other hand, are aimed at drying up the source of drugs, cutting off the illegal drug supply so that drugs will not be available. Those who favor supply-side tactics believe that the United States' growing hunger for drugs has been created by the people who supply them. They believe that the mere availability of drugs creates demand. Supply-side tactics include the spraying of illegal fields of coca, poppy, or marijuana with herbicides that kill the plants, the destruction of illegal drug processing labs, the seizing of illegal drugs on their way into the United States, and the arrest of drug distributors and pushers.

Supply-side tactics are more difficult to carry out because destroying or seizing the drugs before they reach the consumer frequently requires full-fledged international cooperation, which many foreign countries are unwilling, or unable, to provide. Supply-side tactics are also far more costly than demand-side tactics because they include the use of enforcement agents, high-tech surveillance apparatus, and weapons, as well as payments to foreign countries for such things as aerial spraying, training and supplying foreign enforcement agencies, and foreign aid.

Stopping illegal drug trafficking is an extremely complex

problem with no easy answers. Those who support demand-side tactics think the government wrongly favors supply-side tactics. They believe that making demand-side programs a priority could end the drug problem without having to depend on foreign cooperation. They maintain that if the U.S. government channeled the money it now spends on supply-side tactics into prevention and rehabilitation programs, greater gains could be made in winning the war on drugs.

Unfortunately, according to recent research cited in *Newsweek* magazine, demand-side tactics work, but only up to a point. The most effective preventive education programs, for example, succeed with only 50 to 60 percent of their participants. At least 40 percent, the rest of the participants, remain unconvinced. That 40 percent is what makes a drug crisis. Rehabilitation also works only some of the time. The best programs may boast a 50 percent success rate—that is, half of the addicts who go through these often lengthy and expensive drug treatment programs get off and stay off drugs. This means of course that 50 percent of those participating in the best programs do not. Experts estimate that up to 90 percent of drug users in less effective programs relapse within six months to a year of becoming drug-free.

In his televised speech to the nation on September 5, 1989, President Bush said that drugs "are the gravest domestic threat facing our nation today." He was voicing the belief of well over half of the citizens of the United States when he said that drugs "are turning our cities into battle zones and murdering our children." President Bush is not the first president to declare a war on drugs (President Reagan also did), but he hopes to mount the most effective offensive. The strategy for that offensive was designed through months of effort by the major government departments involved in fighting drugs, under the leadership of the president's drug-policy adviser, William Bennett. That strategy, recorded in a 235-page policy paper Bennett presented to the president in September 1989, covered all aspects of the drug war, both demand-side and supply-side tactics. The goal is to decrease drug consumption by 50 percent over the next decade.

Today, as we enter the decade of the 1990s, that effort has begun. The government has declared a global war on drugs that reaches from U.S. shores to nations around the world, a war that must target every trafficker and every drug abuser. Demand-side tactics have a part in that war; they can slow the growth of drug abuse. The president has asked for $925 million to treat drug addicts, and an additional $392 million to expand drug education in the schools. Unless America is willing to fight the war against drugs on the demand side, there will always be illegal profits to be made from those who need drugs. As long as there are substantial profits to be made, there will always be criminals willing to take the risk of being caught for the easy money illegal drug sales generate. Effective demand-side tactics are essential to winning the war on drugs.

Had illegal drugs never been available, however, drug abuse could not have begun, let alone reached the epidemic level it has. Successful supply-side tactics can prevent the availability of drugs and end the careers of the hundreds of thousands who grow, process, and distribute illegal drugs as well. Supply-side tactics are equally essential to ending the use of illegal drugs everywhere. The president wants to channel $3.1 billion back to state and local enforcement agencies to help them fight drug traffickers, and to spend $1.6 billion for correctional institutions to house the flood of convicted drug offenders. In addition, he has designated another $1.6 billion for border control and $449 million for foreign aid to cocaine-producing countries.

Fighting the supply-side war on drugs is like fighting any war. It requires the commitment of personnel and money. It takes organization and strategy. It means taking risks and dealing with the results. This book is about the efforts of those in the United States and many foreign countries who are fighting the supply-side war on drugs—citizens, private groups, and officials and agencies at all levels of government. It is a story of helicopters and border patrols, of drug enforcement agencies and undercover police, of politicians and citizens trying often dangerous and sometimes deadly means to stop drugs before they reach the buyer. Those who fight this side of the war on drugs face as complex, elusive, and frightening an enemy as the United States has ever known.

**2
THE
ENEMY**

Consider this: According to an article by James Mills in the *Palm Beach* (Florida) *Post*, the inhabitants of earth spend half a trillion dollars a year on illegal drugs—more money than they spend on food. That figure is three times the amount of money the United States has in circulation.

The illegal drug industry is international. It is also a business bigger than the entire American farm industry or General Motors. In his article, Mills described it as "an empire—sovereign, proud, and expansionist." This "empire" has "its own armies, its diplomats, its intelligence services, its banks, its merchant fleets and airlines." Its most lucrative market is in the United States, where Americans buy 60 percent of the world's illegal drugs.

These drugs—marijuana, cocaine, and heroin—come from agriculturally grown plants. Other drugs, which are chemically created, are also being bought and abused by the ton each year. These synthetic drugs include hallucinogens, such as phencyclidine (PCP or angel dust) and lysergic acid diethylamide (LSD); stimulants, such as amphetamines (speed, uppers); depressants, such as barbiturates (downers); and the so-called designer drugs, such as China White, a drug created by slightly altering the chemical composition of another drug.

Most grown drugs—cocaine from the coca leaf, heroin from the opium poppy, and marijuana from the hemp plant—come from foreign countries, where they are produced and processed deep in the jungles or in remote mountainous regions. The growers are often poor peasants who depend on these crops to put food on their tables, but they may also be drug profiteers whose fields are heavily guarded by men who will shoot anyone who trespasses.

Regardless of where the drugs originate, they are eventually sold to wholesalers who have developed complex smuggling networks to transport their drugs into the United States and elsewhere. Most drugs arrive at major U.S. distribution points such as New York, Miami, and Los Angeles. There drug traffickers distribute their shipments among smaller dealers. They in turn sell portions of their purchase to even smaller dealers and pushers, who sell them on the streets of every American city, town, and village.

The drugs they sell have become increasingly dangerous. The reality of present-day drug use is that a growing number of people are dying from drug overdoses—some the first time they experiment. Drugs derived from plants—marijuana, cocaine, and heroin—are all far more potent and more deadly today than they were even a few years ago:

- Fifteen years ago, only a "drowsy euphoria" resulted from smoking an entire marijuana joint. Today marijuana is ten to twenty times more powerful because of newly developed seeds and improved methods of cultivation. Its main psychoactive, or mind-altering, ingredient, THC, is now at two to three times the level capable of causing severe psychological damage. This includes psychosis, meaning lost or defective contact with reality; mental derangement; and the mental delusions and suspicions of paranoia.

- Fifteen years ago, the cocaine sold on the streets was only 20 percent pure—that is, only 20 percent of the white powder a user purchased was actually cocaine. Today, through increased availability and improved processing, that same packet can be up to 80 percent pure: four times purer, four times more potent. And crack, a derivative of cocaine, averages 75 to 90 percent pure.

- Fifteen years ago, the heroin addict could assume that his drug purchase was only 6 percent pure heroin. Today, Mexican brown heroin averages up to 15 percent pure, while Southeast Asian heroin can sometimes be 60 percent pure. Yet illegal heroin, like any other illegal drug, is not labeled to show its level of purity. Addicts cannot know how to measure a dose, nor can they know they have overdosed until they have injected the drug directly into their bloodstream and it is coursing through their veins. That is why heroin is the leading killer drug, responsible for 1,263 deaths in one recent year.

The new "designer" drugs can be even more dangerous. Created in laboratories by changing the molecular structure of other drugs, "designer" drugs can be 1,000 times as potent as the original drug. Unlike designer clothes, usually the best and most sophisticated available, designer drugs are the cheaply made product of underground chemists out to get rich quick. With an investment of only a few thousand dollars in equipment, for example, these chemists can produce $1 billion worth of the drug 3 methyl fentanyl, a designer variation of a commonly used anesthetic. One gram of 3 methyl fentanyl will produce a million doses at $40 each—and a life of ease for the chemist, who need never work again.

Designer drugs are among the most dangerous substances on the market. Only a few milligrams of 3 methyl fentanyl are deadly. In the brief time it has been on the market, it is known to have caused more than 100 deaths. And because it is hard to

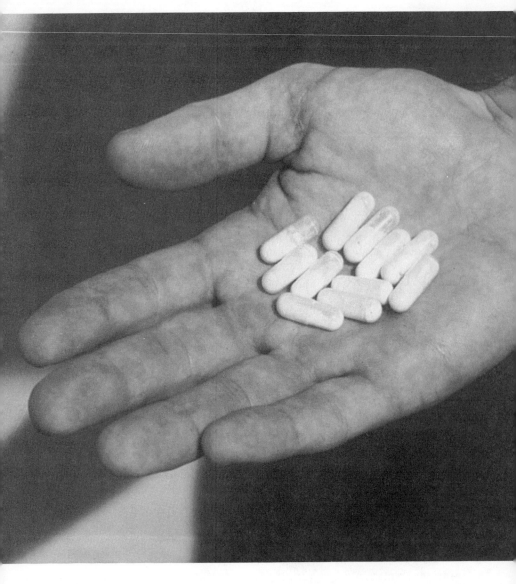

*"Designer drugs" are produced synthetically
in laboratories. Shown here are capsules
of the drug known as "Ecstasy."*

detect in an overdose victim's system, experts believe it has caused many more.

There are no safeguards in the illicit drug industry, and this is doubly true with designer drugs. "The public is taking the role of guinea pigs," said James Hall, chief of the Up Front Drug Information Center in Miami. "These drugs haven't been tested. No one is even sure about the toxic side effects. But people are lining up to buy them."

Whether they are lining up for the first time or the fiftieth, any user of any illegal drug may as well be a first-time user, because the drug he or she is taking is not likely to be the same drug he took yesterday or last week. It could be stronger, it could have a slightly new chemical composition, or it could be "laced" with another drug. And it could be deadly.

### Crack: The New Drug Epidemic
Not only have drugs become more deadly, but many new drugs are more addictive, ensuring that experimenters will become abusers. "Crack," a variation of cocaine, is a compelling example. Drug traffickers created crack to expand the cocaine market, for cocaine had been too expensive for poor or young people to purchase. In 1981, the Drug Enforcement Administration (DEA) began reporting sales of crack in a few major southwestern cities such as Los Angeles, San Diego, and Houston. Sales of crack continued to be localized until late 1985 and 1986, when suddenly the drug became so popular everywhere, from New York to Seattle to Miami, that dealers clamored to get more. Crack is a marketing bonanza. A vial sells for as little as $10, not much money by today's standards. In addition, crack is smoked like a cigarette, a method that appeals to many potential users who would never consider injecting any drug into their veins.

Crack, however, is highly addictive. Users have been known to become addicts within only a few days of steady use, whereas it takes regular cocaine that is sniffed weeks or even months to cause addiction. "With smoked or injected cocaine, a cycle is set up almost immediately—even from the first use for some patients," Dr. Anna Childress of the Philadelphia Veterans Administration Hospital told *Chemical and Engineering News*. "The good feelings are followed so quickly by the bad feelings and the desire for more cocaine that [experimenters] are . . . compelled to search out the drug again."

### Social Costs of Drugs

William Bennett, U.S. secretary of education under President Ronald Reagan and the man placed in charge of drug policy by Reagan's successor, George Bush, said drug abuse can make the user "a lifelong casualty." As the numbers of "lifelong casualties" grow, they present an increasing problem to society. The greater the number of users, the more likely it is that others will be caught in the expanding web of drug abuse. Drug abusers often sell drugs to support their habits. This means they must persuade others to experiment with a drug, hoping to establish "repeat customers" if the experimentation becomes an addiction. Even if drug abusers do not sell drugs, they set a bad example and often exert pressure on others to be "in" or "cool" by using drugs.

The more drug abusers there are, the more burdensome they become to society. This fact is particularly evident in the education system. Young drug abusers affect the quality of education by making it harder for other students to learn. They create many disruptions and distractions in classrooms and hallways. They are rarely interested in academics or school activities.

Drug abusers strain national health and social service resources to the breaking point. They need costly treatment in hospitals and rehabilitation centers. They need shelter, food, and clothing. If they are married, their families need money from welfare, for addicts seldom are responsible enough to hold down a job to support them.

Where there are illegal drugs, there is also crime. Users rob and murder to get the money they need to support their habits. Traffickers protect their territories and struggle for power and profit through frequently violent means. In the period from 1984 through 1988, for example, drug-related violence in New York City led to a staggering five hundred deaths. Recent years have also witnessed the growth of inner-city teenage gangs as drug distributors and pushers. Consequently, in Los Angeles, police made over 12,000 gang-related arrests last year.

Drug-related crime cases have swamped the United States justice system. Enforcement agents made 352,612 busts in 1988, which is 24 percent higher than the previous year. But the federal court system has become so inundated with drug-related cases that judges have to free many criminals. Jails are already seriously overcrowded.

Illegal drugs, the traffickers who profit from them, and those who use them have created such serious problems in the United States that the government will have to budget billions of dollars each year until the crisis can be brought under control. Those billions will have to be raised by increased taxation or by cutting essential programs designed to benefit the young, the elderly, the poor, or recent immigrants. A total war on drugs will require sacrifice on the part of every U.S. citizen.

In addition, those who produce and process drugs—the drug profiteers—pose a serious threat to every nation. They can undermine the moral fiber of society. These criminals use illegal drug profits to gain control of banks, other legitimate businesses, and trade unions. They finance important political groups to protect themselves against discovery or prosecution, and to ensure that local and national laws benefit their businesses. In some countries, drug profiteers have become so powerful that they threaten to "own" those countries—they are quickly becoming the law, the economy, and the government.

Drug profiteers are increasing and thriving because so many people are experimenting with and subsequently getting hooked on drugs. Only a few decades ago, drug pushers were back-alley crooks. Today they are on the streets, in the neighborhoods, in the homes and offices of virtually every sector of American society. Pushers are everywhere because drug abuse is everywhere.

Money allocated to fight illegal drug trafficking has tripled in the 1980s, but during that same time the cocaine supply has increased tenfold. While the U.S. government's antidrug campaign is scrambling to keep up with illicit drug industry growth and expansion, it is failing to stop drugs before they reach the consumer. Cocaine is moving into the United States by the ton, often hidden in the millions of cargo containers that enter U.S. ports each year. The availability of cocaine in U.S. cities and towns has increased so greatly that drug prices have dropped, making drugs all the more affordable.

South American producers, looking for new markets for their drugs, have opened trade networks into Europe, instantaneously increasing the cocaine problem there. Meanwhile, alliances between South American and Asian drug traffickers have streamlined smuggling routes and initiated experimentation with growing opium poppies and the creation of a smokable heroin in South America.

So vast is the drug-trafficking empire that by the day, dreams of destroying it become more unachievable. In 1984, when Colombian police raided a drug processing lab complex called Tranquilandia, it was the largest single cocaine seizure in history. Police confiscated 11 tons of cocaine, much of it already packaged and awaiting shipment. Records showed the lab had been doing a 3- to 4-ton business every month for at least the last seven months. Consequently, law enforcement agents were confident that they had effectively paralyzed the cocaine supply business from Colombia. Yet in 1988, six Tranquilandia-size labs were discovered in Colombia.

Meanwhile within U.S. borders in Tarpon Springs, Florida, police seized 3.6 tons of cocaine hidden in hollowed-out

Brazilian cedar. Farther north, in August 1988, grocery bags stashed in a New York City apartment, imprinted with "Just Say No to Drugs," were found to hold 2.2 tons of cocaine and $2 million in cash. In late September 1989, Los Angeles police located and seized the largest cache of illegal drugs in United States history—20 tons of cocaine worth billions of dollars on the street. That drug bust was followed only a week later in Texas by the second-most important seizure ever made. There, police found 8 tons of cocaine awaiting distribution. Unfortunately, the drug empire continues, unscathed by politicians, police, or governments—and worse, it is growing stronger.

When so many people and so many societies are endangered by a common enemy, the logical question is, how could such a situation occur? Certainly, people recognized the danger of drugs long before the 1980s. In fact, world efforts date back to the turn of the century, when drug abuse first became a major issue. Efforts to ensure that drugs would be used only for experimental or medicinal purposes by controlling the source of drugs are nearly a century old.

# 3
# THE HISTORY OF
# INTERNATIONAL
# COOPERATION

If all the nations and all the people of the world joined in an effort to wipe out every dangerous drug, addicts would have to come to grips with their addiction. This logically leads to a simple conclusion: the primary goal of the war on drugs must be the destruction of the *source* of drugs, preferably in their countries of origin. John Cusack, of the House of Representatives Narcotics Committee, explains: "When drugs are available, they will be abused. Availability creates demand. . . . When you cut the supply, demand dissolves like a dream. . . ."

Representative Cusack's belief is based on earlier efforts, both national and international, to end heroin and cocaine abuse in the United States. When, at the turn of this century, the United States government banned heroin, there were 1 million known addicts in this country. Two decades later, in 1920, that number had been halved. By 1930 it had dropped to 100,000 and by 1940 to 50,000. By the end of World War II, only 10,000 heroin addicts remained.

In the 1880s, cocaine was considered a "wonder drug" and sold everywhere. By the 1900s, however, cocaine's destructive effects led to its being considered the most dangerous of all drugs. Congress passed the Harrison Narcotic Act in 1914, the United States' first important antinarcotic law, and by 1920, cocaine use had also dropped dramatically. Strict customs surveillance at U.S. borders and worldwide controls accepted at a series of international conferences had succeeded in diminishing availability of heroin and cocaine in the United States. These measures, added to domestic social conditions, resulted in a drop in the addiction rate for both drugs.

When, in the 1960s, drug use once again became a serious problem, the government resorted to the earlier tactics it had used so successfully. The government believed that making drugs unavailable would make the problem go away. But times had changed, and transportation technology had become much more sophisticated. The U.S. Customs Service now had more than ocean liners to monitor at the nation's ports. Planes of every size were flying into the United States from all over the world. Thousands of trains, buses, trucks, and cars were crossing U.S. borders from the north and south. The government could not stop drugs from getting into the United States, let alone stop them from being shipped to America in the first place. While throughout the twentieth century United States officials had worked diligently to create international alliances with drug-producing and drug-trafficking countries, alliances aimed at destroying drugs at their source, each year the numbers and varieties of dangerous drugs increased.

### International Agreements
The history of fighting drugs through international cooperation dates back to 1909, when representatives of thirteen nations met in Shanghai to discuss means of controlling illegal drug traffic. Their target was opium. In addition to being the source of illegal heroin, opium is also the source of legal morphine, which has long been used as a painkiller. The goal of these thirteen nations was to work out methods of limiting opium production to the quantities needed for use in scientific research

# PRINCIPAL DRUG SOURCE COUNTRIES

**Marijuana**

Colombia
Jamaica
Mexico
Thailand
United States

**Coca/Cocaine**

Bolivia
Colombia
Peru

**Opiates/Heroin**

Mexico
Afghanistan
Iran
Pakistan
Burma
Laos
Thailand

and medicine. The first binding agreement to establish international cooperation in the control of narcotics used for science and medicine was signed in the Netherlands in 1912.

After World War I, the League of Nations, the international association of countries dedicated to maintaining world peace, became a strong advocate for national laws to control the export and import of opium. Because control laws were not enough to stop the opium trade, the League, in 1936, called for severe punishment of illegal traffickers.

When the League of Nations was replaced by the United Nations in 1945, the new organization established the Commission on Narcotic Drugs to carry forward the League's earlier work. It was at this time that heroin addiction had reached its low postwar level in the United States. Apparently international control measures had been so successful that the government felt assured that drugs could be controlled through United Nations efforts.

The list of dangerous drugs, however, continued to grow. By 1948 UN efforts to control drugs through international agreements included chemically created synthetic drugs, which were becoming a problem. In 1953, the United Nations introduced the concept of controlling drugs by licensing only specific countries to produce opium. Seven countries—Bulgaria, Greece, India, Iran, Turkey, the Soviet Union, and Yugoslavia—were given UN authorization to produce opium for export. Production was to be supervised and enforced by the Permanent Central Opium Board of the United Nations.

In 1961, in an effort to simplify and consolidate all international drug efforts, the UN brought into being the Single Convention on Narcotic Drugs, with an International Narcotics Control Board (INCB) responsible for drug control. The Convention placed coca, the plant from which cocaine is made, under the same production limits as opium. The governments of countries producing coca were obliged to limit production only to medical and scientific use. They were also required to supervise coca fields, license producers, and enforce their laws by punishing offenders and destroying illegal crops.

All the countries participating in the Convention agreed to furnish annual estimates of the drugs to be consumed legitimately and to keep their drug stock and trade within those estimates. The Single Convention also prohibited the ancient practices of smoking and eating opium, chewing coca leaf, and smoking hashish. To allow for the difficulties that would naturally arise from trying to abolish those traditions, the Convention included a reasonable transition period for participating countries.

By the early 1970s, the original group of thirteen nations that had met in Shanghai in 1909 had grown to eighty-five, clear evidence that the problems drugs create were multiplying throughout the world. In 1971 international control was extended to what are called psychotropic drugs—hallucinogens, stimulants, and barbiturates. Some of these drugs were virtually prohibited except for limited scientific and medical purposes; others were controlled through licensing. In addition, because the numbers and varieties of dangerous drugs continued to grow, the World Health Organization (WHO) was designated to research and decide whether new drugs should be covered by the controls already imposed on old ones.

In spite of UN efforts, drug use and abuse increased alarmingly during the 1970s. In 1981 the UN General Assembly outlined a revised four-part strategy to improve its international drug-control program. This strategy called for (1) wider adherence to international treaties, (2) coordinating the antidrug efforts of all nations, (3) eradication of drug crops and productions, and (4) development of programs that encourage farmers to grow legal crops.

### Wider Adherence to Treaties
The United Nations strategy called for wider adherence to existing treaties because all nations had not been fully meeting their

obligations to honor the agreements that had been signed throughout the twentieth century. In support of this effort, the United States threatened to withhold foreign aid from nations that did not honor their antidrug obligations. When the Bolivian government failed to make a determined attempt to curtail its illegal drug production, the United States withheld $8.5 million of the $72 million it had budgeted for aid to Bolivia.

In Pakistan, martial law had kept illegal drug production to a minimum. After President Zia ul-Haq died and the government relaxed martial law, production resumed, increasing until the United States, which furnishes Pakistan with about $350 million in foreign aid, put pressure on the government to do something about illegal production. In addition, under the provisions of the Anti–Drug Abuse Act of 1986, the United States continues its pressure on drug trafficking nations. The act provides for a system under which the president must certify each year that a foreign country receiving U.S. aid is either cooperating fully in combating narcotics production and trafficking or taking steps of its own to deal with illegal drugs.

### Coordinated Efforts

The United Nations antidrug strategy also called for coordinating international efforts to balance the supply and demand for drugs, including those related to illegal drug production. Many world organizations have agreed to share their information in order to increase drug fighting activities. To provide reliable information on illegal drug activities, the U.S. government has given the collection of data on narcotics production and trafficking top priority. For example, one extensive cooperative effort, Operation Chem Con, aims at stopping the diversion of ether and other chemicals essential to the processing of coca leaves into cocaine, and opium plants into heroin. By monitoring and limiting the amounts of ether imported for legal production, cooperating nations make it very difficult to obtain ether illegally. Even when drug traffickers can buy ether, they must pay prohibitive prices. The 55-gallon (208-liter) drum of ether that drug producers could once buy for around $200 now costs $8,000. The U.S. Drug Enforcement Administration (DEA) has also sponsored conferences such as the International Drug Enforcement Conference (IDEC) Series to encourage dialogue among nations on effective antidrug strategies.

The DEA has also done more than provide information and training for countries that need drug enforcement help. Operation Snowcap, a three-year multinational effort, was implemented in 1987 to disrupt South American cocaine production. DEA agents, for example, worked with the Bolivian police to intercept smugglers' trucks and seize the chemicals they needed for coca processing. If coca is not processed within four days, it rots. Operation Snowcap in its first two years resulted in the dismantling of 240 cocaine laboratories and the seizure of 1.2 million gallons (4.5 million liters) of chemicals used to make cocaine. By breaking the supply chain, the operation made harvested coca worthless because it could not be processed. If the seizures continue, the price of the coca leaf will drop below the break-even point for Bolivian farmers, making it more profitable for them to plant legal, rather than illegal, crops.

### Crop Eradication

The third part of the United Nations strategy is cooperative eradication of illicit drugs and drug traffic. To encourage compliance with this strategy, the United States has promoted programs such as aerial spraying of illegal poppy, coca, and marijuana fields with herbicides. In many cases, the U.S. government has also furnished other countries with the necessary planes and chemicals to accomplish the task.

However, ecologists and scientists concerned about the long-range effect of herbicides on the environment have questioned the wisdom of crop eradication. Herbicides are chemicals that inhibit or destroy a plant's ability to survive. Unfortunately, while these chemicals may destroy whole fields of illegal drugs, no one is sure how dangerous their chemical residue is or how long it will last in the soil. Spike, for example, is an herbicide that the U.S. government has tried experimentally and wants to employ for wide-scale use. It is, officials maintain, nontoxic and the least environmentally worrisome of the herbicides available for use.

Unfortunately, according to *Sierra* magazine, even Spike's manufacturer, Eli Lilly & Company, refuses to sell it for the purpose of destroying fields of illegal drugs. *Atlantic* magazine reports that Walter Gentner, ex-chief of the U.S. Agriculture Department's Narcotics Laboratory, resigned to protest the government's use of Spike. He believes the government is taking a "cavalier attitude toward the potential environmental hazards of Spike." Spike is so controversial that in Peru's Upper Huallaga Valley region, leftist guerrillas called the Shining Path, an organization bent on overthrowing the government, surrounded and captured a fifty-man garrison and shot its officers to retaliate against even limited spraying. While the Shining Path's motives are political rather than environmental, their leader, Abimael Guzman, could blame the Peruvian government for allowing the spraying, which, he said, "even the Yankee monopolies admit is like small atomic bombs."

The only alternative to spraying illegal drug fields is destroying them by hand or machine, virtually uprooting the bushes one by one. The Special Project for Control and Eradication of Coca in the Upper Huallaga (CORAH) sends its 462-man force to complete this tiresome task when an illegal field is discovered in Peru. CORAH employees are paid $73 a month for their work, which is always dangerous. Thirty-four CORAH workers have already been murdered by either guerrillas or traffickers.

Eradication can also include destroying drug stockpiles after they have been harvested and the labs where traffickers process drugs to prepare them for export. Through Operation Blast Furnace the U.S. government provided 160 soldiers and civilians to ferry Bolivian antidrug forces on 256 raids on suspected cocaine labs. By working with cooperating nations that do not have the equipment to locate and destroy illegal drug fields and labs, the United States has helped to undermine illegal drug profits. U.S. drug enforcement officials have also trained foreign antidrug agents in effective methods of surveillance and seizure of traffickers and their shipments.

### Developing Crop-Incentive Programs
Encouraging farmers to grow legal crops is another strategy aimed at diminishing illegal drug production. In a cooperative program with several South American countries, for example, United States foreign aid paid Latin American farmers $140 for every acre (0.4 hectare) of legal crops such as corn and wheat they planted. This incentive program, which spent $18 million in 1988, is designed to make legal farming more attractive. Researchers are also developing new varieties of seeds that are especially suited to drug producing climates and soils or that produce greater numbers of crops per acre. By increasing the profitability of food production, the United States hopes that farmers will choose to grow legal crops.

### Freezing Assets
During the United Nations convention on drug trafficking in 1988, forty-three nations developed provisions for freezing the bank accounts of those accused of drug trafficking and for confiscating the money of those found guilty, wherever they reside, thereby crippling the traffickers and preventing them from resuming their business once they have been released from prison.

### Effects of
### International Agreements
The United States has had some success in its attempts to create international alliances, both through the United Nations and through treaties with countries in Europe and Central and

*Bolivian farmers harvesting wheat.
The U.S. has developed an incentive
program to encourage farmers in several Latin
American countries to grow legal crops.*

South America. In 1972, for example, Turkey was the main source for the opium used to make heroin for the U.S. market. With the support of the United States, the Turkish government tightened its opium harvesting and processing procedures and enforced its new laws with strict penalties, and as a result, opium production fell. Another success occurred in Mexico, which had replaced Turkey as the major source for heroin in North America. Mexico was also a major supplier of marijuana. In a joint effort with the United States that began in the mid-1970s, Mexico reduced production by spraying its illegal marijuana and poppy fields with herbicides that killed most of the plants.

These two successes, however, were bittersweet. Although Turkey is no longer a worrisome source for illicit opium, it remains a major trafficking route for heroin. And recently, according to the Narcotics Committee of the U.S. House of Representatives, Mexico's "marijuana production has come back. Heroin manufacture is increasing and the quality and quantity is increasing." In addition, Mexico has become an important transit point for cocaine entering the United States.

Although the United States has cooperated in all international antidrug efforts, changing conditions throughout the world make the drug problem different today from what it was in the past. For the most part, efforts to gain international cooperation in the war on drugs have resulted in failure. These efforts have not destroyed the plants that produce agriculturally grown drugs. They have failed to catch all of the producers, the refiners, the wholesalers, and the international smugglers who make up the illegal drug industry. And they have failed to unite the countries of the world in effective action against all forms of drug trafficking.

# 4
# FACTORS IMPEDING
# FOREIGN EFFORTS

When it comes to pointing the finger for failure to end the drug crisis, many U.S. politicians are quick to blame the South American and Asian countries where drugs are grown and processed. Doing so shifts responsibility for the problem or for workable solutions to other governments. That may save votes, but as one official told Ron Martz of the *Palm Beach Post*, "Blaming foreigners is good politics, but it's bad policy."

According to many experts, Peruvians, Bolivians, and Colombians have been asked to accomplish in their countries what U.S. officials have been unable to do within their own borders. Stopping the supply of drugs in countries with vast areas of isolated forests and great numbers of needy peasants is certainly no easier than stopping the demand for drugs in the United States. Yet "We don't talk with them; we preach at them," Francis McNeil, former U.S. ambassador to Costa Rica, told reporter Martz.

Luis Guillermo Velez, first minister at the Colombian embassy in Washington, D.C., described how disturbed honest Colombians were with their image as "coddlers of drug traffickers." "People in [the U.S.] are not aware of the tremendous efforts in our country, or the number of people who have died in this war on drugs, as you call it," he told the *Palm Beach Post*. As a matter of fact, *Atlantic* magazine reports that many South American officials believe that the cost to and sacrifices of South American countries are dramatically disproportionate to the United States' investment of money and lives. They are angry that South America is paying for fighting the United States' problem. As Colombian president Virgilio Barco told *Time* magazine,

> Every time a North American youngster pays for his vice in the streets of New York, Miami, or Chicago, he becomes a link in the chain of crime, terror and violence which has caused us so much damage and pain. The best help the U.S. could give for the tranquility and the defense of human rights of Colombians would be attacking face-to-face the consumption of drugs in [the United States].

### Widespread Production
Colombia is the source of almost all marijuana and cocaine entering the United States, for even most of the coca produced in other South American countries is processed there. The Golden Triangle in Southeast Asia, composed of Burma, Laos, and Thailand, produces most of the heroin brought into the United States. Mexico is the second largest producer of heroin, and Southwest Asia's Golden Crescent, composed of Afghanistan, Iran, and Pakistan, is third. The widespread foreign origins of these illegal drugs mean that the United States' international efforts must be focused on many countries at once.

The difficulty in controlling drug production is increased by the politics and official policies in the countries where illegal drugs are grown. Not all drug producing countries are friendly to the United States; some, like Iran, consider themselves America's enemy. In other countries, such as Peru, the government

An Indian peasant in the Cauca Valley of
Colombia harvesting coca leaves.

might be willing to work with U.S. officials, but antigovernment and anti-U.S. guerrilla groups like the communist Shining Path, which ally themselves with traffickers, make cooperation difficult.

Despite these difficulties, the United States has succeeded in achieving joint treaties with some nations, among them Turkey, Mexico, Bolivia, and Thailand. These treaties provide for the sharing of information, surveillance of crop production, and crop-spraying programs to eradicate opium, coca, and marijuana fields. Nevertheless, these efforts have had limited success, and the prospects for the future are not hopeful. When one country tries to eliminate its illegal fields, drug traffickers develop new fields elsewhere in the nation or in other countries. For example, when Turkey controlled its opium production, the Mexican traffickers increased theirs. When the Mexican government cracked down on its illegal drug production, the Colombians increased marijuana production to fill the void, making Colombia the world's greatest producer and processor of marijuana as well as cocaine.

### Growth of the Drug Industry
Drug production and trafficking have increased worldwide, and that makes it extremely difficult to seriously damage the industry. The House Narcotics Committee describes Colombia's growing drug trafficking network, for example, as "enormous, highly organized and incredibly sophisticated." Since the 1960s Colombia has also been the processing center for coca leaves grown in neighboring Peru and Bolivia and consequently the main distribution center for illegal cocaine on its way to the United States, Canada, and western Europe. When in 1987 Colombia replaced Mexico as the United States' number-one supplier of marijuana, the Colombians developed more than 23,500 acres (about 9,500 hectares) of marijuana in remote mountainous regions. Today Colombia is responsible for 80 percent of the cocaine and 50 percent of the marijuana entering the United States.

Recognizing the profitable benefits of growing their own drugs, Colombian traffickers have recently developed another 37,000 acres (almost 15,000 hectares) for coca leaf production. According to *Newsweek* magazine as recently as September 1989, while no one is really sure just how much illegal cocaine is being produced in Colombia, estimates range upward from 400 metric tons a year, with sales ranging from $15 billion to $50 billion a year.

The production and trade of coca leaf continues to expand. Colombia's neighbors, Peru and Bolivia, are the two largest growers of the coca leaf. Coca-growing in Bolivia was legal until early 1988. Farmers grow coca leaves for chewing and for use in tea. But while the Bolivian government now limits legal coca production to 24,000 acres (almost 10,000 hectares), illegal coca farming is thriving. In 1987, approximately 100,000 acres (about 40,500 hectares) were devoted to coca, and in 1989, despite the new law, that number grew to 106,392 acres (43,000 hectares).

Peru's president Alan Garcia Perez sarcastically calls the drug trade "Latin America's only successful multinational." By that he means that the drug industry is the only Latin American industry making profits worldwide. In fact, the drug trade is so profitable that most producing countries in Latin America are economically dependent on it, even though drug profits rarely stay in the producing countries. The $800 million in annual profits that do remain in Peru are twice what it earns from copper, its major legal export, and in Bolivia cocaine exports earn $200 million *more* than all Bolivia's legal exports combined.

At the same time that the trade in marijuana and cocaine is thriving in South America, several Asian countries are doing a brisk business in heroin, which they process from raw opium. The opium trade in Asia has existed since the nineteenth century, when the drug was used as barter for spices, tea, and silk. Despite international efforts, that business continues to flourish.

Iran is one of the world's largest producers of opium. (Ironically, Iran's religion, Islam, prohibits the use of opium, and Islamic laws require the death penalty for possession of the drug.)

In March 1989, the Bush administration asked the Afghanistan rebel government in exile to curb opium cultivation in areas under guerrilla control if it expected assistance in its own reconstruction efforts. According to the *New York Times*, rebel leaders have failed to issue a promised decree against farming opium. Afghanistan is the largest producer of opium in the Golden Crescent. In Pakistan, also, manufacturing and trafficking of opium have increased in the last few years.

Nigerians operating out of the Golden Crescent complicate matters, according to one official quoted in *Editorial Research Reports*, because their organization is the only one that covers four continents. "They control their product from its purchase in India or Pakistan, bring the stuff to Africa and then take it to Europe and the United States," he said.

In the Golden Triangle, in Southeast Asia, strained or nonexistent diplomatic relations with Burma and Laos make cooperation in the war on drugs very difficult. In 1989 the U.S. government added Laos to its list of drug-producing and drug-trafficking nations disqualified from receiving American aid. Finally an optimum growing year and Burma's preoccupation with internal political problems will mean that the Golden Triangle's ability to supply opium and heroin to the rest of the world may increase as much as 20 percent by 1990.

These South American and Asian countries are currently responsible for most of the world's illegal drugs, but the names and places can and do change. Small plots of coca plants exist in many Latin American countries where chewing coca leaves has long been accepted. Indian farmers have always grown the plant for their own consumption and see nothing wrong with the practice. When drug kings encourage these small farmers to increase their production by paying them what seems enormous amounts of money for coca, the farmers have every reason to do

A soldier cuts down poppy plants, the
source of opium, as part of an
eradication program in Thailand.

so. Large-scale drug production is spreading quickly to Brazil, Ecuador, and Venezuela, and to Jamaica and other islands in the Caribbean.

As the profits reaped by drug traffickers grow, production of illegal drug crops increases. The drug trafficking networks strengthen because the benefits of quick riches appear to outweigh the dangers of criminal prosecution. When one government steps up its drug eradication programs, there are always poor people in other countries willing to increase their production for the dollars it will bring them.

## The Economics of
## Drug Production

Most drug producing countries have a history of unstable economies. Their people are poor, and many scratch out a living from a few acres of land. The average income in most Latin American countries, for example, is $2,000 a year; yet a Bolivian farmer who plants coca can make from $2,000 to $4,000 a year from a single acre (0.4 hectare). "We couldn't live if it weren't for coca," said one farmer.

Bolivia is one of several Latin American countries cooperating with the United States in the "crop substitution incentive" program. This program seeks to make food crops such as corn more profitable than drug crops. Bolivian farmers are paid $140 for every acre of legal crops they plant. While this is certainly a bonus, it is a far cry from the profits gained from growing coca. The 35,000 Bolivian farmers who produce coca earn a combined income of $100 million, ten times what they could earn growing any other crop. As long as this trend continues, the message is clear: those who grow illegal drugs are far better off than honest farmers.

In addition to providing profits to farmers, drug production means jobs. In Bolivia, officials estimate that one-fifth of the entire labor force is involved in drug production and processing. In Colombia, 222,000 coca farmers and 74,000 paste transporters supply 300 drug exporters. From growers to drivers to buyers to messengers to guards to accountants to traders—a whole army of people numbering in the millions are gainfully employed in the drug industry. Because their survival is dependent on their jobs, they see the illegal drug industry as a good thing. For these workers, and for those who envy their standard of living, economic reality blurs the line between right and wrong.

The attitudes of the general public in these countries change when those who profit most from the drug trade shrewdly use some of their earnings to provide food, housing, or education for the poor. To those in need, they seem like Robin Hoods, and the poor protect and even love them. According to the *New York Times*, several drug bosses have gained respectability by buying up huge tracts of land and siding with local farmers against leftist guerrillas, creating a new image for themselves as "pillars of the anticommunist establishment."

Jose Gonzales Rodriguez Gacha, a well-known drug baron, used another tactic by raising the salaries of the inhabitants of his hometown near Bogota, Colombia, with his drug earnings. In 1982, the people elected Pablo Escobar Gaviria, another known drug king, as alternate deputy in the lower house of Colombia's Congress. Escobar, whose estimated wealth is $4 billion, had become Robin Hood to many Colombians by providing education, housing, and a public zoo for the people of the city of Medellin. In 1989, Paraguay elected Andes Rodriguez, a general linked to illegal drug trafficking, as their president.

The economics of the drug industry, however, reach beyond the level of workers who worship Robin Hoods. The big "bosses" and their untold wealth have a profound effect on the economies of their countries. Not only do they own great ranches and fleets of cars and airplanes, but in many countries they come close to "owning" the economy itself. Their billions are invested in the very organizations on which the economy is based—the banks, the industries, and the unions. The bosses use their illegally obtained money to buy legal companies and financial institutions that then generate legal profits. In this way, drug money is "laundered," or made clean and legitimate.

In essence, the laundered drug money disappears into the country's economy. This creates problems for two reasons. Although the businesses financed by laundered drug money function as legitimate businesses, they often compete unfairly with the truly legitimate businesses not owned by drug bosses. For example, a drug-owned air cargo company can temporarily undersell other companies until they are driven out of business. Once the competition is bankrupt, the drug-owned cargo company has a monopoly. It can then charge outrageous prices, and its clients have no choice but to pay. In addition, when the amounts of drug money being pumped into the economy are so great, most businesses and all the workers those businesses employ are "owned" by the drug bosses. This is exactly what has happened in such countries as Bolivia, Colombia, Peru, and Panama.

### The Power of the "New" Drug Bosses

Growing richer and richer, drug bosses soon wield their power in other ways. Once they can control the economy, they can make puppets of politicians. No politician remains popular if people are out of work because mines are shut down. No politician can count on the support of farmers who cannot get their products to market because truck or railroad strikes have disrupted the transportation system. No politician can stay in power if people cannot buy food because strikes in the shipping industry cut off supplies of necessities. Thus in a surprise raid on the ranch of well-known drug trafficker Hugo Anez in Bolivia, for example, it was no surprise when antinarcotics agents found Anez having lunch with a Bolivian senator. Because the drug bosses have the power to make things happen, politicians sometimes cultivate illicit friendships that benefit both the politician and the boss.

The new drug bosses are criminals of the highest order who have united to increase both their power and their profits. Called the "Coca Nostra" in South America, they are visible, and because of their enormous power and wealth, they are untouchable. Their drug trafficking businesses handle anywhere from 2,000 to 10,000 pounds (900 to 4,500 kg) of pure cocaine a month. Monthly sales range from $20 million to $70 million.

According to Richard Merwin, whom the U.S. State Department hired as a civilian to join the department's Narcotics Assistance Unit (NAU) team in Bolivia a few years ago, the law consistently avoids these bosses of the underground drug empire and focuses instead on "the mass of impoverished peasants that makes up the empire's work force." "The bosses," he reported to *Atlantic* magazine, own "TV stations, cattle ranches, and other businesses, they operate small fleets of aircraft out of major airports, their addresses are in the phone books, and their whereabouts at any time are probably not too difficult to ascertain." As Merwin points out, "If someone wanted to get them, it would be easy to do." Yet they are left alone, allowed to operate openly. Often they proudly flaunt the wealth everyone knows is derived from illegal drugs. One reporter for the *Atlantic*, for example, watched several of the biggest traffickers "betting tens of thousands of U.S. dollars in cash on a single cockfight."

In some countries, drug bosses are so safe from prosecution, so above the law, that in many areas they become the law. In Asia the power of a drug boss can bring a violent end to those who oppose him. Khun Sa rules the Golden Triangle of Burma, Laos, and Thailand, and his word is law. According to *U.S. News and World Report*, deserters from his organization "are tracked down and shot, informants buried alive [and he] orders wrongdoers hanged, drawn and quartered in the marketplace of Ban Hin Taek, his former Thai headquarters village." Under his power are 15,000 "well-equipped, highly disciplined men under arms." Both the Burmese and Thai armies have made several attempts to "dislodge" Khun Sa, but their efforts have always failed.

In Bolivia, often called the "grandfather of the cocaine industry," most of the richest and most powerful bosses were wealthy cattle ranchers and soybean and sugar farmers in the early 1970s. Together with a corrupt military, which was using public funds to buy land for cocaine production, they became an elite class in Bolivian society. That elite consisted of about twenty organizations, most buying paste from locals or nearby Peruvian farmers, processing it into pure cocaine base, and selling it to exporters in Colombia.

When a government does try to crack down on the drug trade, however, the bosses have the means and methods to disappear until the manhunts pass and things calm down. This is presently the case in Colombia, where President Virgilio Barco has declared war on the drug trade. According to reporter Joseph Contreras of *Newsweek*, several of the Colombian drug bosses are "haunted, rarely sleeping in the same bed for more than two nights in a row. They travel behind elaborate cordons of security men." They also depend on tip-offs from government officials they have bribed.

These men are the major exporters and smugglers of cocaine. They have united, creating the "Medellín cartel," named after the city of Medellín, Colombia. Their cartel numbers between five and ten organizations that, according to *Newsweek* magazine, "must be regarded as among the best-organized, most lucrative and most violent criminal enterprises of modern times." Yet while it is organized, it is also a "loose and constantly shifting set of underworld groups that share both risk and profit; almost anyone can play. . . ." The cartel is extremely vicious and vengeful. When one *Newsweek* reporter wondered whether the Mafia, long known for organized crime in Europe and the United States, might try to take over the cartel, a federal lawman laughed. "Don't worry about that," he said. "The Colombians would blow 'em out."

Colombian drug bosses have organized their cartel for

several reasons. Often member groups specialize in a particular aspect of drug trafficking. One group simplifies the purchase of coca paste in Peru and Bolivia, another guards shipments headed for Colombia, and another controls the final processing into cocaine powder and readying it for shipment. Another group specializes in murder. Medellín is home to hundreds of professional hit men. Sometimes bosses enter into business ventures together or share inventory. The most specialized part of the process, however, and the part that makes the cartel most mutually beneficial, is exporting the drug to such market countries as the United States. Smuggling requires a complex and extensive network of routes and modes of transportation which must be easy to change quickly should law enforcement agents catch on. In addition, maintaining such a network requires persuading many people to look the other way as drugs pass through or to aid in packaging or transporting the illegal drugs. "It is cheaper for [the cartel] to buy a colonel than for each one to buy him separately," another official told *Editorial Research Reports*.

### Corruption
Bribery, the "buying" of agents or officials who can be useful to traffickers, is widespread. Honest efforts to topple powerful bosses often fail because drug money or drug power has corrupted government clerks and informants, police, and city and national officials. In some countries a local police officer's monthly salary can be as low as $25, and a payoff of $500 is almost as much as he can earn in two years. All he might have to do to earn that payoff is "look the other way" or "make a phone call" if the police are getting too close.

Narcotics Assistance Unit agent Richard Merwin tells of a raid on a drug-processing lab that was delayed twenty-four hours, supposedly because the antinarcotics agents' planes lacked fuel. Whether the fuel was not available or whether Merwin was purposely delayed is unknown, but when the raiding party finally did arrive at the remote lab, only a few pounds of the cocaine, some money, a small plane, and two low-level traffickers were still there. The bosses had probably been tipped off by one of the captains in the raid. Within a few days, that captain was driving a new Mercedes Benz he claimed he had purchased on his $75-a-month salary. As for the two low-level processors, they were released from jail a few days later when the judge cited "irregularities" in another antinarcotics agent's paperwork. The agent made the errors in return for a gold Rolex watch.

U.S. officials may also be tempted with bribes. Richard Merwin, who operates in Bolivia, reported that one captured narcotics boss said to him, "Tell you what, my friend. I'll give you a check, and you fill in the number of zeros you want. OK?" Merwin refused, but only two days later, the boss was released by a judge who himself had probably been bribed by drug traffickers. "I have to tell you," said Merwin of the antinarcotics enforcement structure in Bolivia, "I think that a hundred percent . . . was corrupted." Certainly the corruption goes to the highest levels of government. Occasionally the situation seems more hopeful. In 1986, for example, the Bolivian interior minister was fired for receiving payoffs from the coca bosses, but such actions are rare. And the higher the corruption goes in government, the more dangerous it is for anyone to try to fight drug traffickers.

### Retaliation

When corruption does not work, drug bosses can call on their hired guns to persuade their opponents to cooperate with them. The Colombian cartels call it *plata o plomo*, "money or lead." Small armies of henchmen threaten and even assassinate anyone who dares stand in a trafficker's way. In Bolivia, Richard Merwin's family suffered power outages and the knifing of the family dog before his own assassination was ordered. He left Bolivia before the order was carried out, but other drug enforce-

*Soldiers discover a jungle cocaine-processing
lab on Bolivia's "coca route."*

ment agents the world over have not fared so well. U.S. Drug Enforcement Administration agent Enrique Salazar "Kiki" Camarena was tortured and killed in 1985 in Mexico. Twenty-two Mexican policemen were also killed in another, single incident.

Perhaps nowhere has retaliation become more threatening than in Colombia, where drug bosses run a regular school for motorcycle-riding assassins, called *sicarios*. Their trainers have been hired mercenaries, professional terrorists and soldiers who owe no allegiance to anyone. The drug barons are also equipped with the finest, most sophisticated arms, an array of weapons capable of matching those of the Colombian army.

Most experts agree that the Colombian democracy is fighting for its life. According to *Newsweek*, Colombia "is locked in a ferocious struggle to maintain the rule of law. . . ." To help outsiders understand the enormity of the crisis in Colombia, George Church of *Time* compared what is happening in Colombia to a similar but imaginary scenario in the United States:

> Try to imagine drug gangsters murdering both Attorney General Dick Thornburgh and his predecessor, Edwin Meese. Next, pretend that drug triggermen and guerrilla allies rub out almost half the Supreme Court—say, Justices William Brennan, Byron White, Antonin Scalia and Sandra Day O'Connor— along with hundreds of lower-ranking but still prominent jurists. Expand the list of victims to include *Washington Post* editor Ben Bradlee and Los Angeles police chief Daryl Gates, both slain, and Amy Carter, kidnapped and held briefly as a warning to authorities who might get tough with the narco-barons. And then the grand climax: the 1987 assassination of George Bush, murdered at a campaign rally just as he had become the favorite to be elected president the following year.

*Time* goes on to list the fate of Colombian officials and citizens who had the temerity to speak out against traffickers: 178 judges shot; twenty-four members of the Supreme Court killed by guerrillas who were probably hired by the drug barons; two successive justice ministers shot, one of them fatally; an attorney general, the police chief of Colombia's second largest city, and the editor of a major newspaper all killed; a former president's son kidnapped; and finally, the likely winner of the next presidential election assassinated. Since the summer of 1989, bombings by cartel hit men in Bogotá, Medellín, and other cities and towns in Colombia have become so common that seldom does a day go by without incident or death.

The drug empire in Colombia has become so threatening that attempting to arrest or convict suspected drug bosses requires almost reckless courage on the part of law enforcement officials. The drug empire will fight any attempts to expose it or to punish its bosses. When Colombian boss Carlos Lehder Rivas was arrested for drug trafficking and extradited to the United States for trial in 1987, he vowed that he would have one Colombian federal judge a week killed until he was freed. Lehder is now serving a sentence of life plus 135 years in the U.S. penitentiary at Marion, Illinois.

Yet some experts believe that Lehder is behind bars only because his Medellín cartel associates let it happen; that is, they wanted him out of the organization and out of power. Colombia's recent pursuit of drug cartel leaders Pablo Escobar Gaviria, José Gonzalo Rodriguez Gacha, the most vicious of the kingpins, and Jorge Luis Ochoa Vasquez, however, has prompted broadside threats and outright attacks on many of the highest Colombian officials. So ominous is the situation there that Colombia's minister of justice, Monica de Greiff, resigned in fear for her life and the lives of her family.

The Colombian cartel has made their position clear: "We declare absolute and total war on the government . . . and all those who have prosecuted and attacked us. . . . We will not respect the families of those who have not respected our families [and] we will burn and destroy the industries, properties and mansions of the oligarchies." Signing their threats "The Extraditables" because the U.S. government wants Colombia to capture them and send them to the United States for trial, the group has adopted the slogan "Better a Tomb in Colombia Than a Jail Cell in the U.S."

The Extraditables have become so ruthless that in September 1989 their men were targetting the families of security forces members. Assassins gunned down the wife of the police commander of Villa Maria de Caldas on September 4, 1989, and the wife of an army colonel in Bogotá on September 5, 1989. The drug barons have also tried to silence the media, making many reporters and publishers afraid to speak out. Four employees of the newspaper *Vanguardia Liberal* were killed on October 16, 1989, when a bomb destroyed the newspaper's building. The newspaper's publisher doubted that *Vanguardia* could continue publishing.

Despite the danger, Colombian president Barco has stated, "We will not be cowed. We shall prevail over the forces that would destroy our democracy and enslave our nation." After the murder of presidential candidate Luis Carlos Galan in August 1989 and the public outrage that followed it, President Barco proclaimed a state of siege. That allowed him to arrest and extradite accused drug traffickers requested by the United States. President Barco ordered Colombian police to round up any trafficking suspects, and in one weekend alone the police arrested over eleven thousand people. Unfortunately, the twelve men most wanted by the U.S. attorney's office, among them Escobar, Ochoa, and Gacha, had already escaped into hiding.

## True Costs of a Drug Economy

Illegal drug profits may seem, on the surface, a boon to poor economies. But except for the income of illegal drug farmers and local traffickers, more than 70 percent of the illegal profits land in foreign banks. No taxes are levied on this money; consequently, no benefits go to the poor who need them most. Those who have grown rich through drug profits spend most of their money on luxury items, creating an even greater separation of the rich and poor. Drug bosses who masquerade as Robin Hood, buying schools and zoos with one hand while robbing the common people of their liberty with the other, will not always be able to escape resentment from the "have-nots."

The have-nots have other reasons for despising traffickers. For the peasant, life would not be possible without farming. Yet coca farming is destroying good farmland. "No other crop in the world causes similar levels of erosion," conservationist Marc Dourojeanni, former head professor at the National Agrarian University in Lima, Peru, told *Sierra* magazine. As a result, "Thousands have . . . died in floods and landslides in the montane jungle region of Peru."

In the rush to provide the world with illegal drugs and to clear rich, new land for more coca, the rain forest of the Peruvian Amazon is being destroyed. Dourojeanni estimated that coca farms, the exhausted lands coca farmers have already abandoned, areas used by peasants who have fled narcotics traffickers, land used by coca growers fleeing police, and land stripped for makeshift airports, camps, and processing labs amount to 1.7 million acres (688,000 hectares). That is one-tenth of all rain forest destruction in Peru in the twentieth century, the majority of it occurring in the last decade.

Not only have coca farmers continued to strip valuable rain forests, afterward leaving the land barren and eroded, but they use herbicides to destroy weeds and increase production, and sulfuric acid and lime to process coca leaves. All are extremely damaging to the ecosystem. As a result, more than 150 streams and rivers in Peru have been polluted by cocaine production.

Damage to the environment is but one of the destructive side effects of drug cultivation. By ignoring or supporting the drug industry, drug producing nations risk growth in drug abuse among their own people. In Bolivia, for example, addiction is increasing rapidly among the nation's youth. Cigarettes laced with coca paste, known as *pastillas*, have made the very substance whose production so many Bolivians support a danger to their own children. Pakistan, an opium-producing country, had virtually no heroin addicts in 1980. By 1983, it had 150,000. In Iran, the world's largest producer of opium, the government of the Ayatollah Khomeini jailed addicts and executed traffickers. Nevertheless, recent statistics indicate that Iran has as many as a million opium addicts and 100,000 heroin addicts. Colombia reportedly has a higher per capita addiction rate than the United States.

The pattern is the same in other drug-producing countries and in countries that serve as transit points for drugs on their way to other countries. Southwest Asian heroin travels through the Soviet Union and other Eastern Bloc countries. Historically, their communist governments have claimed drug addiction was only the "curse of the capitalist world," and that they had immunity to such decadent habits as drug abuse. Unfortunately, no country seems immune. The Soviet Union, Poland, Hungary, and Yugoslavia now have their own share of addicts. In April 1989, the Soviet Union agreed to discuss cooperation with the United States on terrorism and narcotics trafficking.

Drug-producing countries have also experienced an escalation in the violence against officials who oppose the drug trade. When Colombia increased its antidrug efforts in 1984, the traffickers responded by assassinating one of the country's most powerful critics of the drug trade, Rodrigo Lara Bonilla, the minister of justice. Enrique Arenal, director of drug control for the attorney general of Mexico said that in Mexico City alone, forty-six people assigned to drug control have died fighting drugs in the last six years. The Mexican army now has one-fourth of its forces, about 25,000 men, assigned to full-time drug eradication and seizure.

These problems have caused grave worries in Latin America. Most Latin Americans look on the drug trade with anger and dismay. The majority do not approve of the drug profiteers and recognize the problems drug trafficking creates. As *Atlantic* reporter Gustavo Gorritti makes clear, most have only contempt for the "crude gangsters" who they fear "will seize control of the society."

As years pass and the problem only increases, foreign and United States officials are realizing that adjustments will have to be made if supply-side tactics are ever going to win the war on drugs. Jeffrey Sachs, a Harvard economist, told *Atlantic* that "Our [the U.S.] government was negligent not to have studied the economic aspect . . . to come to grips with the coca economy and the human realities it creates." Help must be well planned and carefully directed, with everyone knowing exactly what must be accomplished and who will be responsible.

More money is also needed if drug trafficking is to stop. In the past, U.S. foreign aid to Latin America and the Caribbean amounted to only 70 percent of U.S. aid to Egypt. President Bush's plan is to triple the amount of money allocated for South America to $261.2 million. In addition, the president's drug plan proposes $2 billion over the next five years. As President Bush's drug-policy adviser, William Bennett, told *Newsweek*:

> It's a long-term process. . . . You can injure major criminal organizations and hamper their effectiveness. But there are 250,000 peasants [in Peru]. You are not going to have an overnight change from coca to some other crop. But part of our strategy is to address that . . . with economic assistance over time. It's a long-term economic program.

Economist Sachs suggested cancelation of a cooperating country's foreign debt, extending it new credits from around the world, which could stabilize a poor economy. Money would have to come in the form of programs designed for regional development of coca producing areas. Bolivia, the *New York Times* reported in March 1989, has already begun shifting its priorities away from raids in favor of voluntary crop substitution and eradication. It has asked wealthy foreign nations for $600 million to develop agriculture, build roads, and install electricity in coca regions.

### *"Narco-Terrorism"*

Because the drug industry has become so lucrative, and so entrenched in the countries where it operates, stamping it out is exceptionally difficult. Persuading farmers in poverty-stricken countries to grow other crops may be impossible. Economic dependence on the drug trade and its bosses, along with widespread corruption, means that eradication efforts may always fail. Beyond these problems, however, there is another dimension of the drug trade—drugs as a political instrument.

In the last few years, the U.S. Drug Enforcement Administration (DEA) has noticed connections between leaders of the drug trade and a variety of revolutionaries, terrorists, arms traffickers, political radicals, and officials of several foreign governments. According to *World Press Review,* nearly two dozen countries have been mixing drugs and politics. In Italy, for example, Mauricio Coletti, head of the Italian Communist Party's antidrug campaign, said some time ago that he believed "drug trafficking in Italy has become a political affair . . . linked to every shady movement in Italian politics." In the United States, Miami prosecutors have linked Cuban president Fidel Castro with drug dealers. While Castro did execute General Arnaldo Ochoa Sanchez and three other officers for drug trafficking, many experts believe the move was prompted by a desire to rid himself of rivals for power, not criminals.

Together, the countries involved in some aspect of drug trading and politics stretch from Singapore to Switzerland, Hong Kong to Australia to Panama. In South America, some of

Colombia's estimated $4 billion in annual drug profits is funding guerrilla groups fighting the Colombian army and some is funding the army fighting the guerillas, depending on the location and politics of different bosses. Peru's Maoist guerrilla organization Shining Path also has allied itself with drug traffickers.

Money from drugs can buy arms and support local guerrilla or international terrorist activities. In turn, the revolutionaries and terrorists frequently provide "protection" for the drug industry. They protect crops from narcotics agents. They can, and will, assassinate officials. They can terrorize citizens, villages, and governments on behalf of the drug bosses. Drug money can buy elections for candidates who are sympathetic to terrorist causes, and who then promise protection for the terrorists and drug traffickers, especially in countries that are on shipping routes or are money-laundering centers.

"The drug merchants and terrorists have joined in a deadly marriage of convenience whose only common ground is contempt for democracy and humanity," the *Palm Beach Post* quoted former secretary of state George Shultz in 1988. With the money to support troops and to provide the best in military arms, even the smallest terrorist groups can become fearsome foes. U.S. law enforcement officials are worried about the recent growth of availability of military-type automatic weapons such as AK-47s, M-16s, and Uzi submachine guns, which they believe are being purchased with drug money. In April 1988, when U.S. agents broke up a Chinese heroin ring in New York City, they seized 1,000 M-16s headed for Libya, a Mediterranean country with strong anti-U.S. sentiments.

It took some time for the U.S. government to realize exactly what was happening. Carlton Turner, former White House drug-policy adviser, told *U.S. News and World Report*, "Nobody worried about narco-terrorism—particularly the State Department—because it was dirty business. . . . No one looked at the big picture. It was disheartening." The big picture was "disheartening" because the web of dirty business entangled many governments, including the United States.

## The "Noriega" Affair

The case of General Manuel Noriega of Panama revealed the extent to which the United States was caught in the web of drugs, dictators, and narco-terrorism. For some time, U.S. officials had known not only that Noriega was a brutal dictator but that he was sympathetic to drug traffickers. Under his protection, drug bosses were smuggling cocaine through Panama into the United States while laundering their profits in Panama's banks. The United States government, however, apparently needed Noriega for its own "not so legal" operations. Through Noriega, the U.S. Central Intelligence Agency (CIA) operated an electronic surveillance station in Panama, "eavesdropping" on both South and Central America. Noriega also allowed Panama to be used for the training of Contra rebels from Nicaragua, rebels many U.S. officials supported, and money destined for the Contras from unauthorized U.S. sources was allowed to pass through Panamanian banks.

According to Newsweek (15 Jan. 1990), Noriega knew the U.S. government needed him and took advantage of the situation. He became personally involved with the drug trade. Drug traffickers paid him handsomely for his help. He was making millions by taking a cut of their profits. If one of the traffickers crossed him, however, he tipped off the Drug Enforcement Administration and put the dealer on a plane to Miami, where the DEA could arrest him. Noriega also allowed DEA agents to capture small drug-laden boats in Panamanian waters, while at the same time protecting the biggest shipments, from which he took his cut. Noriega played the United States off against the drug traffickers so well that the DEA considered him a champion of drug enforcement. In May 1986, John Lawn, director of the DEA, thanked him for his "vigorous anti-drug-trafficking policy." In response, according to *Newsweek*, Noriega bragged "about making a monkey of the DEA."

It was not just with drugs that Noriega made "a monkey" of the United States; he was also deeply involved politically with countries of the Soviet bloc. Noriega helped Cuba and Nica-

Former Panamanian dictator Manuel Antonio
Noriega was allegedly heavily involved in
drug trafficking and money laundering.
A U.S. invasion of Panama ousted him.

ragua get around U.S. trade embargoes that forbade the importation of their products. He allowed the Soviet spy agency, the KGB, to establish headquarters in Panama City, thereby allying himself with communist forces. Finally, he provided weapons to several groups unfriendly to the United States, including Nicaragua's Sandinistas.

It took some time before the U.S. government realized that Noriega's drug trafficking was funding the very revolutions that threatened democracy in the Western Hemisphere and that, according to *U.S. News and World Report*, his "combination of drugs and terror [had] become an unofficial new weapon . . . of several Soviet-bloc nations bent on destabilizing the West." "Drug trafficking produced a very good economic benefit which we needed for our revolution," a Nicaraguan diplomat who defected to the United States in 1983 testified. "We wanted to provide food to our people with the suffering and death of the youth of the United States."

When the DEA finally realized the extent of Noriega's duplicity, the United States indicted Noriega for drugtrafficking. The U.S. government then moved to freeze all Panamanian assets and impose economic sanctions on the country. According to an agreement made with Panama, Noriega was supposed to step down in September 1989, but not surprisingly, he remained in power. In October 1989, a coup attempt led by Major Moises Giroldi failed, and Giroldi was captured and executed. Finally, in December 1989, U.S. troops invaded Panama and deposed Noriega.

According to many experts, the Noriega affair was another example of the U.S. government's turning its head from illegal activities, even drug smuggling, when it needs something done. In 1974, Victor Marchetti and John Marks wrote a book about covert operations and the Central Intelligence Agency, one of the government's most important data-gathering organizations. *The CIA and the Cult of Intelligence* maintains that the CIA overlooked one tribe's production of opium in the Golden Triangle because the tribe was "needed" in the war against communism. That tribe trafficked heroin to Vietnam, where more than 25,000 U.S. servicemen became regular users of the drug during the Vietnam War. "The agency would hire Satan himself as an agent if he could help guarantee the 'national security,'" Marchetti and Marks wrote.

The CIA denies that it has ever condoned illegal activities, but retired admiral Stansfield Turner, director of the agency under President Jimmy Carter, admitted to *Palm Beach Post* reporter Ron Martz that on occasion, some agents had, in fact, ignored drug trafficking activities in certain "sensitive" cases. "One gets the impression they [the CIA] used these kinds of people in the past," Turner said.

In April 1989, a two-year investigation by a Senate subcommittee did report that the Reagan administration had sacrificed anti-drug-trafficking efforts in order to achieve other political priorities in Nicaragua, the Bahamas, Honduras, and Panama. The report concluded that the administration "overrode programs to keep drugs out of the United States" because it seriously underestimated the threat to national security posed by drug traffickers.

Whether in the use of drug profits for revolutionary or guerrilla activities or for terrorist activities or for covert operations, drugs and politics have become a factor in the history of drug trafficking. Politics have given drugs new purpose, especially in the countries where poverty breeds revolution. It is politics that must stop the illegal drug trade and end drug abuse, but it is also politics that make doing so an increasingly difficult world problem.

### Is International Cooperation Possible?

So far United States foreign aid has done little to save economies "owned" by drug kings and corrupt officials. The assistance of U.S. drug enforcement agencies has done little to damage more than a few soldiers of drug trafficking. As one DEA agent in Bolivia told *Post* reporter Ron Martz, ". . . you can't go back home and say we're winning the war on drugs because the only people we're really hurting are the *campesinos* (farmers)." With only a few exceptions, the big bosses remain unharmed. The use of military troops and equipment has had little success except to cause suspicion about the United States' role in other countries' affairs. The crop incentive programs have not paid enough to persuade coca farmers to switch to legal crops, and herbicides have stirred environmental controversy. Drug-crop production is spreading everywhere.

Although cooperation among nations is critical in fighting the war against drugs, the results have generally been disappointing. The nations that have signed agreements with the United States and promised adherence to the United Nations' antidrug strategies have been unable to successfully combat drugs. Joint strategies have focused on drug eradication, crop substitution, and law enforcement, but as criminal problems. In addition, according to *Atlantic Monthly,* all of those strategies focus on capturing and jailing traffickers and destroying their assets. South American jails were filled to capacity and courts drowning in drug cases years before similar problems arose in the United States. "After ten years of continuous effort," the *Atlantic Monthly*'s reporter Gustavo Gorritti writes, "the failure of this approach is evident. No judicial or law-enforcement system in the world can suppress an activity in which whole societies and national economies are engaged."

A country's politics, its economy, the will of its own people are all factors that can undermine the best-intentioned efforts. When a nation's resistance to eradication efforts sets citizen against citizen, governments back down.

In Bolivia, for example, an entire village turned out ready to battle its own government's agents who were there on a drug raid. To avoid bloodshed, the government called the agents back. After the raid, a Bolivian general said, "Cocaine is too much an American problem and not enough of a Bolivian problem for Bolivians to be killing Bolivians."

In Peru, peasants are violently against efforts to eradicate their coca. Many have allied themselves with the communist Shining Path for support, helping the guerrillas become stronger and a greater threat to the Peruvian government. Peruvian army officials fighting the guerrillas refuse to go after drug traffickers unless they are clearly associated with the Shining Path. One army official told *Time*, "Don't ask us to go against the people growing coca."

Often, strong antidrug measures have only succeeded in increasing the strength of the drug industry. In Peru, drug traffickers used government officials and their agencies to dispose of drug trafficking competitors. On the other hand, governments trying to quell revolutions and at the same time catch and punish drug traffickers have instead pressured the two groups into partnerships that only make them harder to stop.

### Using Force

According to President Bush, the new U.S. drug strategy will increase law enforcement support in countries such as Colombia and Bolivia. U.S. agencies such as the DEA, the FBI, the Customs Service, the Coast Guard, the U.S. military, and the CIA will expand their services to governments in need of help. Increasing the role of those agencies, however, must be done with caution. Police actions against farmers only anger the population and make otherwise honest people support the traffickers. Anti-U.S. sentiments are also strong in many Latin American countries; increasing U.S. involvement in foreign efforts against traffickers could backfire, placing some unstable governments in jeopardy with their people or straining the alliances the U.S. was attempting to strengthen.

Not only must the U.S. government be careful not to alienate foreign nations, but it must also be careful to maintain public support at home. U.S. citizens are wary of getting involved in foreign wars on foreign soil; no one wants another Vietnam War, which severely divided the country in the 1960s and 1970s and resulted in the loss of thousands of U.S. soldiers' lives.

*A shipment of American helicopters
arrives in Bogotá, Colombia,
to help fight the drug war.*

Military options the Bush administration has researched include increased naval interception, commando raids, and ground troop prevention of massive shipments of illegal drugs. According to *Newsweek*, many experts believe that it would be simpler and more efficient to stop planes leaving Colombia than to intercept them at U.S. borders. By using AWACS surveillance planes, which are airborne radar stations, or by stationing a Navy fleet off the Colombian coastline, the United States could monitor outgoing planes or boats and intercept them. So far, however, the Pentagon is wary of the cost, which would be in the hundreds of millions of dollars, and of the possibility that mistakenly bringing down a suspicious plane might result in an international incident.

Commando raids, or "surgical strikes," could be effective, but planning and training for such strikes would take a long time, and drug lords are equipped to replace destroyed labs almost immediately. Troops on the ground could disrupt and even destroy the supply side of the cocaine trade, but the area that troops would have to monitor is approximately one-fourth the size of the United States. Most of it is isolated jungle terrain. According to *Newsweek*, the Joint Chiefs of Staff are reluctant to commit U.S. soldiers to accomplish what Latin American armies should do themselves. "In Vietnam we couldn't beat a Stone Age enemy," a senior military official told the magazine. "This is a Star Wars enemy." In September 1989, the White House did disclose that a "small band of Americans will be dispatched to train the Colombians in the use of the military equipment they will be getting." William Bennett's aides, however, told *Time* that "American soldiers will not go out on raids or act as field commanders [as they did] in Vietnam."

While the government and politicians are cautious about sending U.S. troops to help fight or arrest drug traffickers in Colombia or other major Latin American drug export centers, American citizens' attitudes about such involvement have changed dramatically. The Gallup Organization conducted a poll for *Newsweek* in late August 1989 which found that 53 percent favored U.S. involvement, despite the fact that 64 percent expected that increased involvement would result in increased violence against Americans by traffickers. *Newsweek* reported that one Pentagon official responded to this apparent public approval of sending troops to countries such as Colombia by saying, "There is no shortage of would-be Rambos who think all it will take is a few well-placed ambushes. Everybody's looking for the magic formula, the quick fix."

The Bush administration and the DEA are pushing the completion of a secure base in Peru for Operation Snowcap, which plans search-and-destroy missions on drug traffickers' labs, airstrips, and warehouses. There, both the Peruvian National Police and U.S. drug enforcement agents will work together to attack the supply line. President Barcos of Colombia wants to increase international controls on the chemicals, such as ether and acetone, that traffickers need to process coca. Both efforts will require U.S. staff.

### Targeting the "Kingpins"
Targeting the big traffickers and corrupt officials might also disrupt the flow of drugs. Called "decapitation" because it cuts off the heads of trafficking enterprises, this strategy will be a part of President Bush's offensive. Attorney General Thornburgh says, "Seize their drugs—they've got an assembly line [and] they can roll more drugs out. You take [a drug boss such as an] Ochoa, an Escobar, a Gacha or a top money launderer out of the operation, and it disrupts them."

An example of the "decapitation" strategy was the capture by Mexican authorities of accused cocaine trafficker Miguel Angel Felix Gallardo in April 1989. Gallardo had been wanted for more than ten years, yet had continued to operate openly because he paid off police officials. At the same time Gallardo was captured, Mexican officials arrested eighty police officers, "virtually the entire force of Culiacan," Gallardo's hometown.

Colombian law enforcement agents, on their part, are now searching for their most powerful drug bosses.

Nicaragua has proposed a new plan that would unify Central American efforts to stop illegal drugs. The plan proposes that centralized drug enforcement authorities in every country streamline drug enforcement activities. In addition, "special attachés" responsible for drug-related issues would be assigned to each country's diplomatic missions, thus increasing communication among nations about illegal trafficking and other countries' antidrug plans and activities.

Drying up the source of drugs in foreign countries will be absolutely necessary if the United States government is ever to put an end to illegal drug trafficking. How to do so, however, is still unclear. No program in any country has as yet proved so successful that it can be used as a model for future programs. Crop incentive programs need further work to be truly attractive to poor farmers. Crop eradication programs create hostilities, endanger agents, and, with the use of herbicides, endanger the environment as well. Using law enforcement agents to destroy labs and capture processors can be effective only if the government wholeheartedly supports the effort. This requires that corrupt officials will no longer be tolerated. Pouring money into foreign economies has served only to increase corruption in the past. New programs will have to be carefully monitored to ensure that foreign aid is spent constructively.

# 5
# PROTECTING
# U.S. BORDERS

- In October 1988, an Eastern Airlines employee in Miami finds 56 pounds (25.5 kg) of cocaine left aboard an L-1011 jet that had recently arrived from Colombia.
- In February 1989, U.S. agents capture 800 pounds (about 360 kg) of heroin and confiscate $3 million in cash belonging to a Chinese heroin ring. They arrest New York Chinatown businessman Fok Leung Woo with eighteen other members of the ring.
- On September 5, 1989, the Customs Service seizes 25 tons of Middle East hashish concealed in a false compartment of a ship docked on the Columbia River. The drugs are valued at $150 million.
- In October 1989, 871 pounds (395 kg) of cocaine worth $40 million is found in a truckload of California and Washington apples.

Because international cooperation has failed to halt the production of drugs, the borders of the United States are besieged. In a period of one year, the incidents above, reported by the *New York Times*, are but a sampling of the hundreds of raids and

A U.S. Customs Service agent prepares
for a mission. The Customs Service
has an impressive fleet of aircraft.

seizures made by law enforcement officials across the country. Traffickers walk or drive in with drugs from Canada in the north, and, in far greater numbers, from Mexico in the south. Drugs come by ocean liners and high-speed pleasure craft into major ports, onto deserted beaches, into small towns along rivers, and into the deserted swamplands and bayous of the southern seacoast. Drugs arrive on everything from jumbo jets at major airports to single-engine planes that land on rural airstrips and open fields.

The United States enforces the laws that regulate the use of drugs within its boundaries. Once illegal drugs are within the jurisdiction of the United States, the government can confiscate them and arrest, try, and punish the traffickers. So varied are the entry points and so imaginative the smuggling techniques, however, that despite many successful seizures, enforcement officials miss at least 90 percent of the drugs coming into the country.

The government's effort to stop drugs in transit before they reach American-based wholesalers is called *interdiction*. The target of interdiction is the air, sea, or land transportation system that illegal suppliers use to ship foreign drugs to wholesalers in the United States. Interdiction reduces the amount of illicit drugs entering the country and consequently the amount being transported within U.S. boundaries. Of course, any drugs that are prevented from reaching illegal wholesalers are also prevented from reaching their main destination—the drug users. Interdiction occurs not only outside U.S. borders, but also inside, after drugs cross U.S. boundaries. Interdiction efforts are bound by international as well as by U.S. laws.

### Agencies Involved
### in Interdiction
The chief agency in charge of interdicting drugs and apprehending traffickers at U.S. ports of entry is the Customs Service. The Coast Guard is the primary U.S. maritime enforcement agency

*Interdiction, or stopping the flow of drugs before it reaches American shores, is a major element of the overall "supply side" strategy to combat drugs.*

and the only one with jurisdiction on the high seas. Customs and the Coast Guard have joint jurisdiction within the 12-mile (19-km) limit.

Another agency involved in interdiction is the Drug Enforcement Administration (DEA), an arm of the Justice Department. It was created in 1973 through a merger of various antidrug agencies. The merger's purpose was to centralize the U.S. drug law enforcement effort. The DEA's long-term goal is to paralyze and destroy drug trafficking organizations by catching their leaders and confiscating the money and valuables these organizations need to function. The head of the DEA performs his job under the general supervision of the director of the Federal Bureau of Investigation (FBI) and the U.S. attorney general.

The DEA has offices in dozens of foreign countries and in every state of the Union. It is the only federal agency whose sole mission is drug law enforcement. Consequently, the DEA leads America's war on drugs wherever the battles occur. While it has no police powers abroad, the DEA is responsible, under policy guidance of the State Department and U.S. ambassadors, for programs associated with foreign drug law enforcement. It also supervises the surveillance of drug trafficking in foreign countries and the training of foreign and U.S. antinarcotics agents. The DEA's information and expertise therefore is crucial to stopping drugs at U.S. borders.

Within the jurisdiction of the United States, the DEA not only works independently but often coordinates the drug enforcement efforts of other agencies. It works with such federal agencies as the U.S. Customs Service, the FBI, the IRS, and the military; with federal, state, and local "task forces"; and with state and local police. The DEA trains agents from many of these organizations in all aspects of drug traffic investigation, including the surveillance and infiltration of drug rings.

The DEA cooperates closely with the Customs Service to stop drugs at the border, while the FBI helps both the DEA and

Customs by gathering and reporting facts, locating witnesses, and compiling evidence against the drug traffickers. All three agencies "make," or prepare, cases independently or in cooperation with one another. Once a case has been made, the Narcotic and Dangerous Drug and the Organized Crime and Racketeering sections of the Criminal Division of the Justice Department can prosecute the high-level drug traffickers and see that their drug-related assets are forfeited.

In addition, the government has set up special assignment groups of the Justice Department, the DEA, the FBI, the Customs Service, and other federal agency personnel. These task forces target specific drug trade areas, such as Florida, a major port of entry for illegal foreign drugs. The South Florida Task Force is a good example of how interdiction can work. It was set up in Miami in 1982 because Miami was, and still is, bustling with drug trafficking activities. For the past several years Colombian refiners, who are responsible for the majority of illegal cocaine entering this country, sent most of their drugs through Miami. Eventually they replaced American drug wholesalers with their own men. Although edging out the former wholesalers required gangland beatings and executions, "owning" this part of the operation gave Colombians an even greater share of the drug profits. In a sense, Miami became the Colombians' "foreign office." It was, according to one journalist, the perfect place for the U.S. government to take a stand.

Once targeted, Miami became a city under surveillance. The object was not only to capture incoming drug shipments and smugglers but to arrest the people who ran the operations: the bosses, refiners, and wholesalers. The program required constant surveillance of suspects. It set up infiltrators who could then "leak" information about shipments and meetings. The Coast Guard, the Customs Service, and harbor patrol police checked incoming boats of all sizes. Helicopters patrolled the oceans beyond U.S. jurisdiction to sight offshore cruisers, the "mother ships" from which smaller boats could pick up partial shipments. Air patrols and radar located smugglers' planes. Black

Hawk helicopters and tracking aircraft followed and forced down suspicious planes. On the ground, accountants sniffed out tax fraud and money-laundering operations, and lawyers and judges saw to it that, once arrested, traffickers were sent to jail.

The agents, prosecutors, patrol boats, and helicopters assigned to the South Florida Task Force have been effective. Seizures of heroin increased 1200 percent, and seizures of cocaine, 986 percent. By 1984, seven times more illegal drugs had been captured than in 1980. "If you thought of the United States as a patient, there were a lot of bloody spots," Carlton Turner, President Reagan's drug policy adviser, said of the new enforcement program. "But in South Florida you had an artery that was severed." As recently as March 1989, the program led to indictments of thirty people, among them Pablo Escobar, José Rodriguez Gacha, and Fabio Ochoa, well-known members of the Medellín cartel, by a federal grand jury in Jacksonville, Florida. Although few of these men have been captured or brought to trial, the task force's work has made them the target of Colombia's largest-ever manhunt.

### The Effect of Interdiction Attempts

Drug seizures and criminal prosecutions of drug traffickers hurt drug rings. Every seizure costs them profits and men. The smaller traffickers face the constant danger of bankruptcy when a cargo is lost, stolen, or seized, for a single shipment can be worth several million dollars. Three or four lost shipments can break a small distributor. The larger traffickers, however, are harder to put out of business. Their assets are such that they can withstand many seizures before beginning to feel the loss. To prepare themselves to withstand serious loss, they simply increase the supply they have available for shipment. According to Admiral Daniel J. Murphy, chairman of the National Narcotics Border Interdiction System's coordinating board, while "our efforts have increased and our seizures have increased, [so has] the supply available for importation. . . ."

Not only have the drug suppliers increased the production

and shipment of drugs, they have also found new ways to out-smart the law. One is to switch their smuggling routes to other areas. Instead of concentrating their operations in Miami, Colombians now route some of their drugs through Mexico, up the East Coast, or along the Gulf Coast. With thousands of miles of uninhabited shoreline, bayous, and swamps, the Gulf Coast states have been a smuggler's paradise since the time of the famous pirate Jean La Fitte. There, even bulky marijuana can easily be slipped in on small boats.

Drug traffickers are also utilizing the most modern and sophisticated technological equipment to outsmart narcotics agents. Not only do they have access to private planes and boats; they have equipped them with radar and radio frequency scanners, enabling the traffickers to track and avoid drug enforcement agents who might be following them or monitoring a trafficking route or area. When an illegal shipment of drugs is "dropped" on land or sea, it often has attached to it a locator beacon that will simplify finding the shipment offshore, in secluded bayous, or in dense forests.

Enforcement agents also have to patrol some 2,000 miles (3,200 km) of border between the United States and Mexico. Texas, New Mexico, Arizona, and California borders have long been vulnerable to illegal immigrants sneaking into the United States, but today they have become the route of drug traffickers as well. The problem has grown so severe that in January 1989 the U.S. Immigration and Naturalization Service recommended building a ditch along the U.S. border with Mexico in a desert area where drug smuggling is probably the most serious. A report issued by the Federation for American Immigration Reform has recommended a 50-mile (80-km) chain link fence to deter the invasion of illegal aliens and drugs.

While such tactics might diminish the smuggling problem in one area, 50 miles of fence will barely begin to barricade the rest of the border between the U.S. and Mexico. In addition, smugglers do not always come by land. "We're literally being invaded by land and sea," said former Texas governor Mark

White in 1985. Smugglers have also built airstrips in rural Mexican areas and farmlands only a few hours from the United States, making their day and nighttime flights easier, cheaper, and safer. One law enforcement agent described the atmosphere on the border as "sinister," so saturated with drug traffickers has it become.

Smuggling activities have also increased along the eastern coastline of the United States. Some air shipments now land in the farmlands and forests of Georgia, and drugs float into the U.S. through the salt marshes of the Carolinas and farther north along the Virginia and Delaware coastline.

Having moved some of their ports of entry away from Florida, traffickers have also been relocating their centers of operation. Even in the tiny mill town of Central Falls, Rhode Island, smugglers managed to set up one of the biggest cocaine distribution centers in the United States. Wholesalers employed as textile workers were grossing $100 million a year in drug sales. Los Angeles, however, is a favored center for many drug refiners and wholesalers. Like Miami, Los Angeles has access to the sea, a major international airport, proximity to Latin America, and the large banks necessary for investments and money laundering. Yet with air shipments possible to nearly any city, drug operators could relocate again if government narcotics task forces made it too difficult to do business in Los Angeles. "It's just like building a sand castle. You build a good wall here, the sea doesn't come in. It starts going in somewhere else," said William Von Raab, U.S. Customs commissioner.

Not only are drug rings operating in new cities, they are also smuggling drugs that are more profitable and more easily concealed, cocaine in particular. Since cocaine is less bulky than marijuana, it is easier to conceal and is worth more per pound.

### Other Tactics
Another tack smugglers are using is the development of new methods of concealment that are more difficult to detect. For

A U.S. Customs Service surveillance screen
for monitoring offshore craft.

example, U.S. postal inspectors have found marijuana and hashish concealed in Express Mail packages from the Virgin Islands. A different kind of "air mail" shipment is being dropped by parachute, often at night and in remote areas of Georgia, Florida, Louisiana, and Alabama.

Drugs have always been concealed in such things as furniture, fruit, aircraft engines, hollowed-out books, and automobile spare parts. Today they are concealed in more unlikely imports. In 1988, a Chinese drug ring operating out of the Golden Triangle tried wrapping heroin in cellophane and inserting it in the bodies of live goldfish bound for an importer in San Francisco. Drugs have arrived in heroin-spiked shampoo, in bean-sprout-washing machines from Hong Kong, in false-bottom suitcases, in cassettes and records bound for music stores, and in diapers. They have been concealed in the soles of shoes, in beer cans, and in containers-within-containers of toxic chemicals, and huge quantities have been sealed in large containers marked "Anchovies in Salt Water."

Drugs are also carried across borders or through customs by hired smugglers called "mules." Although mules are nothing new, the increase in their number and variety is. They come from all walks of life, from airline pilots to salesmen to tourists. Often they have no idea who hired them and only a telephone number to call when they arrive at their destination. Capturing a single mule does almost nothing to help enforcement officials trying to arrest a major trafficker. Unlike the interception of planes and boats loaded with millions of dollars' worth of drugs, the arrest of a mule is a "small bust" at best. Probably for this very reason, refiners and wholesalers are using mules more often.

Interdicting illegal drugs requires constant surveillance and far more agents than the DEA and other groups have available. "We don't have enough people to look at even a tenth of the container traffic that comes in here," one frustrated agent told the *Palm Beach Post*. To aid interdiction efforts, the U.S.

government has allowed the armed services to cooperate with enforcement agencies, an involvement that has been forbidden since the Civil War, and added 600 new DEA and FBI agents along the Mexican border. Additional congressional legislation has provided the funding for enhanced intelligence collection and special interdiction aircraft and radar for U.S. Customs and the Coast Guard. In September 1988, U.S. Customs purchased four P-3 Airborne Early Warning Aircraft, which can provide a radar network capable of detecting smugglers from the sea or air. With all of the additional surveillance equipment the planes will have on board, their cost will exceed $100 million.

Despite increased personnel and technical equipment, U.S. senator Paula Hawkins of Florida estimated that 10,000 aircraft per year elude border agents. "That averages out to about two drug planes per hour penetrating American airspace." Furthermore, an even greater number of boats slip into U.S. harbors and mules walk through customs.

It is estimated that between 90 and 93 percent of the foreign-produced drugs destined for American streets eventually get there. Admiral Paul A. Yost, commandant of the Coast Guard, told the *New York Times* that U.S. law enforcement agencies are stopping only 7 percent of the cocaine smuggled across the border.

While interdiction has been well financed and seizure of illegal shipments increased more than 2500 percent between 1981 and 1987, more drugs than ever are crossing the nearly 20,000 miles (32,000 km) of U.S. borders. Illegal drug traffickers and their huge, well-organized rings make guarding those miles by land, air, and water "logistically impossible and financially foolhardy," said Florida's governor Bob Graham. "If we have declared war, we have thus far lost it."

A 1986 report titled *The Border War on Drugs* completed by the congressional Office of Technology Assessment came to the same conclusion several years ago. Not only would stopping drugs at our borders require manpower and technology beyond the resources of any government, but also the increased surveillance would probably slow the United States' import and tourist businesses to a halt. In the long run, most U.S. citizens would eventually find the invasion of their privacy required to truly capture drugs crossing the border an unforgiveable and unacceptable infringement on their own rights.

The drug strategy designed by William Bennett and proposed by President Bush in September 1989 cuts the budget for interdiction activities by $80 million, leaving approximately $1.6 billion to fund the men and equipment needed to intercept drugs on their way into the U.S. While interdiction was the Reagan administration's primary drug-trafficking strategy, it is clear that the new administration no longer sees interdiction as its most important weapon.

On the other hand, if the United States is to set an example for foreign nations, it cannot ignore the drugs crossing its borders. Interdiction remains a necessary step in the process of decreasing the flow of drugs.

# 6
# STOPPING
# U.S. GROWERS
# AND PRODUCERS

Deep in a vast California forest that is considered one of the United States' national treasures, a four-wheel-drive Jeep quietly makes its way through the dim undergrowth and comes to a stop a few feet from an isolated patch of emerald green bushes. Strangely, while the area surrounding the patch seems ancient and untouched, the ground surrounding the bushes has been recently cleared and cultivated.

In an Oregon national park, two park rangers carefully pick their way closer to a similar patch high on a mountain slope overlooking thousands of acres of timber. They are looking for booby traps.

Two private citizens, Paul Clark and Dickie Tynes, were not as careful. When they set off a booby trap while turkey hunting in Arkansas's Ouachita National Forest, Clark thought his friend's shotgun had misfired. "The next thing I knew I was flying through the air," Clark told Frances Hunt of *American Forests* magazine. The blast threw Clark 10 feet (3 m), blowing off part of his finger, breaking his foot, and leaving him covered with cuts and bruises on his arms and back. It also created a hole in the ground 3 feet (0.9 m) wide and 1 foot (0.3 m) deep.

Clark and Tynes were but two of the private citizens who in recent years have had the misfortune of stumbling upon an illegal marijuana patch. Other hikers and hunters have been threatened and shot at in isolated areas from the East to the West Coast and from Texas to the Canadian border. Illegal drug traffickers have set up business in the United States' rural areas, and they are serious about succeeding.

### A "Growth" Industry

DEA surveillance estimates indicate that U.S. marijuana farmers are doing business in a big way. Although interdiction has failed to stop the main flow of drugs at the borders, it has been successful enough to have the unforeseen effect of encouraging marijuana production inside the United States. Because it is more difficult and expensive to smuggle bulky marijuana into the country, the market for homegrown marijuana has blossomed. Today the United States has the dubious honor of being the third largest producer of marijuana in the world.

It is not surprising that homegrown marijuana has become a major industry. U.S. marijuana is of the same or better quality than foreign competitors' products, and it is cheaper. While Colombia and Mexico produce more of the drug, U.S. growers do not have to deal with the high costs of smuggling, giving them the edge over their foreign competitors. Marijuana is also grown in so many areas of the U.S. that, once harvested, the 20- to 50-pound (9- to 23-kg) bundles of plants need to change hands only a few times before reaching the street. This eliminates the need for several middlemen.

Generally, most of the marijuana growing areas are in the South and West, primarily because of the geography—huge, thinly populated areas. The canyons and ridges in these remote areas are perfect for illegal marijuana operations. The soil and light are also excellent for marijuana plants. Finally, vast stretches of farmland or timber and limited enforcement personnel make surveillance of trafficking activities very difficult and

A *federal drug agent shows former attorney
general Edwin Meese part of a haul of
marijuana plants seized by agents in
Ozark National Forest in Arkansas.*

detection unlikely. The Midwest, however, also ranks high in marijuana growing, with Indiana being the state with the greatest number of ditch weed—wild, uncultivated plants— destroyed in 1988. Hawaii, however, led all states in the number of cultivated marijuana plants destroyed in 1988, and Tennessee placed second.

Traffickers plant most of their marijuana crops on private land, but in the last decade many have begun using public lands for cultivation. National parks have reported some illegal marijuana plots, but national parks bustle with visitors during growing and harvesting times, making it harder for traffickers to remain anonymous and undetected. Land Management areas in Oregon, California, New Mexico, and Arizona are definite trouble spots too.

But it is in U.S. national forests that traffickers have chosen to do most of their growing. The land belongs to the U.S. taxpayers, not the grower, so that discovery of a "patch" can lead to the arrest of the grower only if he happens to get himself caught harvesting it. In 1980, only 5 percent of the domestic marijuana crop originated in national forests, but today that figure is now 20 percent, worth $1 billion on the streets. Marijuana is growing on 32,000 national forest acres (about 13,000 hectares) and forcing officials to place almost 1 million additional acres (404,700 hectares) under "constrained management" because they are unsafe for tourists, hikers, hunters, and forestry personnel.

Marijuana cultivation in the United States has had a short history. Many of its first illegal farmers were young people who were disenchanted with society, authority, and law enforcement during the late 1960s and early 1970s. They dropped out of society, moving to rural farms to live alone or in communes. Many of them believed drugs had mind-expanding capabilities. Others saw nothing wrong with smoking marijuana to relax. These people were products of the drug culture of the sixties, and many had little regard for laws they believed were unjust. At first, they grew marijuana for their own purposes, much as the peasants in many foreign countries have grown coca and poppies for their personal use.

But the market for marijuana increased as more people wanted the drug. As the U.S. government stepped up its efforts to stop the flow of all illegal drugs into the country, capturing boat- and planeloads of unwieldy marijuana, many U.S. growers saw the chance to make money by increasing production, improving the crop with new and stronger strains, and organizing the "industry" for greater profits. By 1985, according to the National Organization for the Reform of Marijuana Laws (NORML) a group lobbying for the legalization of marijuana, a record domestic crop of over $18.6 billion made marijuana "the most valuable crop in the United States." Today, a single plant can bring between $2,000 and $2,500 on the street.

As in Latin America, rural pockets of poverty in the United States have become fertile fields for secret marijuana plantations. In Kentucky, North Carolina, West Virginia, Kansas, Hawaii, Oregon, and California—states where the fishing, mining, or timber industries have suffered economic setbacks—major producers of marijuana have stepped up production. Of the 7 million plants eradicated in 1987, the great majority, 79 percent, were located in these seven states. Not surprisingly, many longtime residents of these depressed areas at first hesitated to do anything to stop marijuana production. In towns where business was suffering, growers and dealers paid for "cars and trips with packs of $100 bills," said one resident.

It did not take long, however, for people to become disillusioned with the influx of drug money. Now those who plant for profit are called "greed-heads." "They make it downright unpleasant to live here from August to October," a farmer from Petrolia, California, told one journalist. That is the harvest season for marijuana, a time when growers heavily guard their crops against "patch pirates."

From all over the so-called Emerald Triangle—Mendocino, Humboldt, and Trinity counties in California—come frequent reports of hikers being assaulted or shot at. Trip wires tied to firearms, pipe bombs, and hand grenades guard at least 20 percent of the sites. Enforcement officials have to be painstakingly careful while on patrol. "We simply have not been free to move around in the backcountry as we ought to," Associate Deputy Chief George Leonard says. Growers will maim or murder to protect profits that stagger the imagination. While it may be impossible to accurately determine the actual amount of money involved, experts estimate that in the Emerald Triangle alone, profits had risen to $2 billion a year by the mid-1980s.

Illegal traffickers create danger where rural life was once peaceful, and that danger is not limited to humans. Forest Service Chief Max Peterson reminded *American Forests* reporter Frances Hunt that "Eighty percent of all marijuana sites on national forests are indiscriminately laced with poisons that kill wildlife. Fertilizers are also used and leach into streams to endanger water supplies and aquatic life."

As in every drug-producing country, the profits of illegal drug cultivation create a "bootlegger" economy that benefits only a few people. "They grow it [marijuana] out in the hills and they process it out in the hills. Then they take the money and go to Mexico or the Caribbean over the winter to spend it," said a motel owner in Garberville, California. The longtime residents are left with nothing but increased danger in the woods, increased violent crime, the burden of higher taxes for law enforcement, and lost business because of declining tourism.

### The Eradication Program
The United States government is well aware of the sizable marijuana crops growing in rural farm areas, state parks, and state forests. Officials are also aware that just as the United States is asking foreign countries to cooperate in eradicating their drug crops, it is obligated to eradicate the drug crops within its own borders.

Forty-eight states participated in federally supported efforts to destroy or seize illegal crops in 1989. In California, the program, which began in 1982, is called the Campaign Against Marijuana Planting (CAMP). CAMP is an example of how effective the cooperation of many agencies can be. The Forest Service and Bureau of Land Management allied with twelve federal and state agencies and fourteen county sheriffs' offices to plan and carry out the eradication of illegal marijuana fields and the arrest of drug traffickers in California.

CAMP's effectiveness scores are high. In 1986, it seized and destroyed 117,277 marijuana plants and 1,426 pounds (647 kg) of marijuana buds with a wholesale value of over $400 million. It has arrested ninety-one traffickers and issued warrants for 113 more. CAMP raids have garnered 284 firearms, twenty-seven vehicles, and real property (land and buildings) valued at $4 million. The Internal Revenue Service has also stepped up investigations and prosecutions of traffickers targeted by the CAMP program. They risk indictment for tax fraud and evasion for not reporting their illegal profits.

Enforcement by CAMP and similar programs in other states accounted for the destruction of more than 100 million plants in forty-seven states in 1988. According to the *New York Times*, about 60 percent of the marijuana grown in national forests was eradicated. In addition, in July 1989 New York State introduced the use of the Air National Guard for surveillance of its vast farm- and forest lands. National Guard "spotters" flying in helicopters will locate marijuana fields and then inform state authorities of their location. New York state police will take over from there.

Increased eradication, however, has driven many marijuana growers to try growing techniques that are more difficult to detect. Marijuana plots are highly visible from the air because of their emerald-green color. Growers are now planting smaller plots, tying the plants close to the ground, and using overhanging trees to camouflage them. Others are using garbage bags filled with soil to grow individual plants. The bags can be easily moved about to avoid detection.

In late October 1989, in a coordinated national effort, narcotics agents began cracking down on perhaps the most difficult-to-detect method of marijuana cultivation. Over the past several years, growers have developed indoor marijuana gardens, often in cellars of private homes and in garages, barns, and warehouses. Using artificial lighting and sometimes hydroponic techniques (a method of growing plants in water), growers manage to avoid aerial detection. So successful has indoor cultivation become that mail-order houses specializing in indoor cultivation equipment are thriving. Law enforcement agents have begun using equipment purchase records, and monitoring utility bills that reveal unexplained increases in electricity and water consumption. On October 25, 1989, ABC News reported that several hundred arrests had been made in the last few days, with hundreds more expected in the next several weeks. While this method of sniffing out indoor cultivators is effective, it is both tedious and time-consuming, requiring long man-hours of detective work.

Meanwhile, Congress has passed new laws to aid enforcement officials. Using national parks or forests for marijuana cultivation is no longer merely a misdemeanor; it is now a felony. Those who use booby traps to protect their plots will also face a jail sentence of up to ten years on the first offense and twenty years on a repeat offense. Finally, the secretary of agriculture is now authorized to designate 500 special agents and law enforcement officers to receive special training in drug enforcement techniques and to provide them with the tools— firearms, communications equipment, and surveillance devices —they need to find and catch drug traffickers.

### Drug Laboratories

Another source of drugs within the U.S. is the laboratory. Cocaine is frequently processed within U.S. borders, and crack "labs" are common. Finding the producers of illegal synthetic drugs is another story altogether. The smallest traffickers in synthetics can work out of a bathroom or kitchen. The larger dealers can set up in seemingly legitimate warehouses and garages. Not only can these traffickers operate without drawing attention to themselves, but they can also shift their operations before the enforcement agents on their trail get too close.

Synthetic drugs—LSD, PCP, synthetic heroin, and others —are as dangerous as drugs that come from plants. Synthetic drugs don't need large fields or secluded forest areas to grow. They don't need labor and machinery in order to be harvested. They don't need jungle pits to be pressed and processed, or large storage areas to be readied for shipment. Nor do they need to be smuggled through Customs or dropped from planes. According to *U.S. News and World Report*, synthetic drugs can be created in a lab the size of a closet with a minimum of equipment by anyone "with as little as a college chemistry background."

Synthetic drugs are test tube creations that offer "highs" similar to those of the "natural drugs." Synthetic drugs are known to have caused reactions ranging from temporary paralysis to permanent brain damage to death. They are lethal, yet they are on streets and campuses across the nation. LSD, for example, gained prominence in the sixties and was touted as modern science's "mind-expanding" wonder drug. Dr. Timothy Leary, then a Harvard professor, was among those involved in its early fame. LSD's quick rise to fame is typical of the pattern of synthetic drugs. By the time laws could be passed against its use, it had harmed many unknowing victims and killed others. LSD is still illicitly made and sold.

Ecstasy, or MDMA, is an example of another problem that laboratory drugs create. Ecstasy was a "legal" drug that was sold so openly that it could be commonly purchased in Texas bars. Many experts feared Ecstasy could cause brain damage. When the DEA finally outlawed Ecstasy in 1985, two new "legal" drugs, slight variations of Ecstasy, went into production. Those drugs, Eve and Rhapsody, then kept the illegal drug industry one step ahead of the law. Stopping synthetic drugs poses different problems than stopping agriculturally grown illegal drugs because creative chemists are always devising new mind-altering concoctions, often by changing only slightly the chemical formula or by combining over-the-counter drugs. In the long run, some experts speculate, stopping these drugs may be the most difficult problem the government has faced.

Government efforts to eliminate synthetic drugs have required changes in the law. In 1984, Congress granted the U.S. Drug Enforcement Administration the power to ban, if only temporarily, any drug that becomes a public menace. The DEA then has eighteen months to prove it should be illegal. That law eliminated the need to wait several years while a drug was tested and retested until finally it proved dangerous. Enforcement officials now could ban a drug, force its removal from store counters, seize supplies, and arrest the drug's manufacturer quickly. Unfortunately, in cases such as Ecstasy, illegal drug chemists were able to alter the illegal formula for making the drug just enough to create a new, legal drug that they could sell without risking arrest. Yet the "new" drug still had mind-altering capabilities and was just as dangerous as the original. Congress solved this problem, however, by passing the Controlled Substance Analog Enforcement Act in 1984, which finally gave drug enforcement officials the ability to make the manufacture of suspected drugs and all their variations illegal.

Still, the development, manufacture, and marketing of synthetic drugs continues. New computer-designed combinations of narcotics, more effective methods of using old drugs, and new drug fads make stopping this source of illegal trafficking a nightmare. As one expert stated, "It's a reasonable hypothesis that the more synthetics you have available, the more people are going to play with them."

# 7
# GETTING DRUGS OFF THE STREETS

The apartment's grimy windows overlook the rest of the project —other brick buildings, five floors of other grimy windows. Below, patches of trees and grass surrounded by concrete walkways are littered with broken bottles and crinkled papers. The halls leading to this apartment smell of urine and garbage. Occasionally, a rat rustles in a dim area beneath the stairs, and in the apartment itself, roaches scuttle within the dark, empty kitchen cabinets. Yet according to Mary Cooper in her *Editorial Research Reports* article "The Business of Illicit Drugs," some people think this apartment is the best supermarket in town. It has everything anyone needs to achieve the instant rapture that makes its bare mattress a magic carpet and the bloody scraps of gauze scattered upon it tickets to another kingdom.

This apartment is a "shooting gallery," a supermarket where addicts come to buy and use illegal drugs. In every major city, hundreds of such galleries are run by drug pushers or drug gangs, and they are, according to Cooper, "the last link of a long and largely invisible distribution chain along which illegal drugs pass to users in the United States from producers who are often continents away."

The chain, according to Rand Corporation studies, usually has six U.S. links—that is, six individuals or groups in the United States will handle illegal cocaine or heroin before someone in this shooting gallery ingests it or injects it into his or her bloodstream. Each of the six transactions will make a considerable profit for the seller, so as the illegal drug passes from hand to hand, its value doubles, then triples.

The wholesale level is the first transaction within U.S. jurisdiction. At that level, the government estimates that a kilogram, or "kilo" (about 2 pounds), of cocaine sells for $13,000 to $20,000. By the time a user buys the cocaine, however, 1 gram (0.04 ounce) of it will sell for $50 to $120, two to four times its original price. Along the way from wholesaler to user, four other drug traffickers have made their profits. They are a part of a pyramid of buyers and sellers, growing less powerful but more numerous as each transaction brings the drug closer to the consumer, the casual user or addict.

As the drugs move to each new level down the pyramid, it becomes harder and harder to trace them back to the bosses and wholesalers at the top of the pyramid. The labyrinth of criminal deals created by this system makes it nearly impossible for the police to connect a dead addict with the seemingly respectable businessman in his chauffeur-driven Mercedes Benz who wholesaled the drug several transactions ago.

While one-fourth of all pushers must sell narcotics to friends and family to support their habits, most of the traffickers in the illegal drug pyramid take the risks of arrest and punishment by authorities and the risks of assassination by other underworld competitors for the riches drug dealing can bring. Traffickers believe the risks are worth it. The lowest-level pusher can make $8,000 a week selling 1-ounce (28-g) bottles of PCP; another can make $1 million a year selling crack. "Compare that to working for minimum wage at McDonald's," one policeman remarked in *Editorial Research Reports*.

Pushers come from all walks of life. A seventy-four-year-old

grandmother in Houston, Texas, sold anything from Valium to marijuana out of her home. The owner of a Columbia, South Carolina, ice-cream parlor sold cocaine out of Mr. Yummy trucks. Pushers are sometimes surprisingly "average" citizens. They don't look like criminals, and many times their neighbors would never guess they are.

Some pushers are even prominent citizens, such as the twenty-five New York City physicians and twenty pharmacists caught illegally dispensing prescription drugs to addicts, or the Philadelphia dentist who supplied stockbrokers and lawyers with heroin and cocaine, or the Wall Street stockbrokers who traded cocaine for valuable insider stock tips, or the coproducer of the Broadway play *Checkmates*, or the founder of the Syracuse, New York, chapter of Cocaine Anonymous.

In addition, a growing number of children are pushing drugs. In only four days of February 1989, the *New York Times* reported the arrests of a ten-year-old Hauppauge, New York, youth for selling crack from brown paper bags, two thirteen-year-old boys for selling crack in Roosevelt, Long Island, an eleven-year-old boy who brought over 400 vials of crack to school, and his twelve-year-old brother whom police found at home under the influence of drugs.

Sometimes these children have taken matters into their own hands, selling drugs without their parents' knowledge or despite their parents' attempts to stop them. Even more insidious are the situations in which children are used by their parents or other drug pushers. Because the punishment for being caught carrying or selling drugs is far less severe for children, and because children can operate in and near schools and playgrounds without easily being noticed, they have become a favorite sales force for drug pushers.

*A police raid on a known crack house in Houston, Texas.*

The crack epidemic is not limited to
the poor. Many young "white collar"
workers also use the drug.

### The U.S. Illegal Drug Pyramid

Most illegal drugs originate in foreign countries. Exporters in Latin America or Asia work with importers within U.S. boundaries who accept the smuggled contraband and continue it on its way to the user. The contraband arrives in both large shipments aboard planes and ships and in amounts small enough to be concealed on a single mule. The importer then divides the large shipments or gathers the many small shipments into saleable units destined for other parts of the United States. Major importers seldom have anything to do with small-time operators or pushers. Instead they sell to large-volume dealers or distributors from other areas, who will again divide their purchases for sale to even smaller and less important dealers and pushers. Illegal drug arrangements, or deals, are being made every minute of every day between those on one level of the drug pyramid and those on another level.

The path of illegal domestic drugs—homegrown marijuana and laboratory-produced designer or synthetic drugs—is different only in that an importer is not necessary, since the drugs require no smuggling. Drug distributors and dealers who sell foreign contraband, however, frequently sell domestic drugs as well. Thus the pyramid for domestic drugs is only shorter, with the drugs reaching the user sooner, after fewer transactions, and for less money.

A last source of illegal trafficking originates with perfectly legal prescription drugs made by licensed drug manufacturers. These drugs are the target of all kinds of thieves. Hospitals and pharmacies must be constantly vigilant, for prescription drugs are pilfered by addicts or stolen by drug pushers wherever or whenever the opportunity exists.

A more astonishing and insidious source of otherwise legal drugs, however, originates from the very people entrusted with the drugs, a network of crooked doctors and pharmacists who are in collusion with drug dealers. Dishonest doctors sell illegal prescriptions to drug dealers for $50 to $300 each. They do this by making up phony names for imaginary patients who need the drugs. The dealers then buy the drugs from dishonest pharmacists, giving them the bogus prescriptions to account for their drug sales. The pharmacist sends a copy of each prescription to the state, making everything seem legal, while the drug dealer sells the pills at a great profit. For example, a single tablet of Dilaudid, a painkiller that is sometimes used as a heroin substitute, costs an honest citizen 50 cents. Bought on the illegal drug market, however, that same tablet sells for as much as $55.

This illegal source of prescription drugs is not as easily detected as one might suppose. In fact, few state agencies monitoring the purchase of restricted drugs have the manpower to keep close track of pharmacies or doctors. Computer tracking has been used effectively, however, in California and six other states. The computer can pinpoint suspiciously high quantities of prescriptions from doctors or drug sales by pharmacies, thus tipping off law enforcement officials.

### The Distributors

In the United States, the Constitution protects everyone's right to privacy and protection from illegal search and seizure. Enforcement officials cannot stop and search drug distributors on highways or in trains without what is called "probable cause." That means the police must have good reason to believe that a person or vehicle is carrying drugs. Nor can enforcers burst into a motel or a private home without a search warrant. Before a judge will issue a search warrant, the police must have reasonable certainty that drugs might be concealed on the premises.

Transporting illegal drugs from U.S. entry points to distribution centers has become the occupation of many Americans —small-time amateurs, outlaw motorcycle gangs (over 500 of them nationwide), organized-crime families such as the Mafia, and foreign agents of the drug cartels.

In August 1989, *Newsweek* described another tack both international and domestic traffickers are now using to distribute cocaine. Some have used Federal Express and others the U.S.

Postal Service to avoid possible detection, sending legitimate-looking packages to other traffickers across national and state boundaries. Federal Express has trained its mail handlers to recognize suspicious shipments, turning approximately 6,000 of them over to narcotics authorities since 1979. "It is unfortunate," a Federal Express spokesman told the magazine, "but we are probably the most reliable delivery service. . . ."

One expert believes that the people who previously have been successful in smuggling illegal whisky, or "moonshine," are among the leading drug distributors. This "Dixie Mafia," said Jack Enter, a professor of criminal justice at Georgia State University, "already had the means of transportation. They had the distribution network. I'm convinced that moonshiners with any smarts at all . . . went into drugs." With their privately owned cars and trucks, their network of "friends," their knowledge of the land and of the roads and towns to be avoided, the Dixie Mafia and other organized drug distributors make it hard for drug enforcement agents to track the movement of drugs.

Seizing a shipment of drugs and arresting the carriers is the most obvious, but not always the best, way to fight drug trafficking. Suppose, for example, that agents have infiltrated a distribution ring and know a shipment of drugs is being transported to a distribution center. Rather than seize the shipment, they may choose to follow it in hopes of learning more about the drug network and its leaders. This way they may be able to obtain the evidence they need to destroy the entire drug ring. By waiting and watching, agents have often been surprised to discover that "honest" citizens they would never have suspected are also part of the ring. Waiting also allows enforcement agents to observe the activities of sophisticated operations and to build a case against traffickers all the way back to the most important and powerful leaders.

### Types of Distributors
Using the technique of waiting and watching, drug enforcement agents were able to arrest and get a conviction in Decem-

ber 1988 against the four Chambers brothers, who operated a distribution ring out of Detroit, Michigan. The Chambers brothers also gave agents an opportunity to observe effective organized crime in action.

Billie Jo, Larry, Otis, and Willie Lee Chambers ran their drug empire as well as any Fortune 500 corporation. They controlled 50 percent of all sales in the city. To find cheap help, they recruited young people from the cotton fields in their native Arkansas. They used discount coupons to lure buyers to the most addictive drugs, they manufactured and issued identification cards to their 500 employees, and they ran competitions to motivate their pushers to increase sales. All four are now in jail. Yet their business was so carefully organized that enforcement officials believe underlings have the operation rolling again.

The Mafia, or La Cosa Nostra, whose members are mainly of Italian descent, has long been an importer and distributor of heroin from Europe and Asia, but distributing drugs is merely an adjunct of its other illegal activities. The Mafia gained power during Prohibition, the period in the 1920s when selling alcohol was forbidden in the United States. Once alcohol was again made legal, the Mafia had such a strong foothold in all illegal activities that it merely diversified its operations into gambling, extortion, prostitution, and drugs.

Only recently, narcotics agents working with Italian authorities conducted two major coordinated sweeps against Mafia rings operating in the United States. The "Pizza Connection" was a joint investigation which led to the arrest of hundreds of Mafia traffickers running heroin and cocaine worth millions of dollars to U.S. distributing networks. On the heels of that victory, hailed as the biggest bust in U.S. history at the time, came "Pizza II" and the arrest of 208 suspects in the U.S. and Italy.

The Mafia is only one group making millions from drug trafficking. Others such as the Chinese, the Vietnamese, and the Jamaicans are increasing their power, often taking over traditionally Mafia territory.

Another kind of group, also usually formed along nationality or ethnic lines, is an outgrowth of neighborhood street gangs. These gangs of hoodlums often existed before becoming a force in drug trafficking. Many, like the Crips and the Bloods in Los Angeles, were loosely knit black groups battling each other for power in inner-city neighborhoods. They were violent, they assaulted and robbed, they bribed and extorted, and they marked their territories with the typical graffiti seen in every city. Many were abusers of drugs and pushers when selling drugs was still largely independent and disorganized.

Eventually, however, they seized the opportunity for the big money and power that drug trafficking on the distributor level afforded. They organized and set up sales territories. Today, according to *Newsweek*, gang conflicts have become "a form of urban-guerrilla warfare over drug trafficking." According to the *Palm Beach Post*, the DEA has identified at least 200 gangs in the Miami area alone. Miami gangs range in size from fifty to 500 people. A DEA agent quoted by the *Post* says they are "a virtual army of traffickers," but Miami is just a part of the much larger problem of the big-city gangs that are growing in size and spreading to other, smaller cities.

According to *Newsweek*, the El Rukns of Chicago now number over 12,000 members, some of whom are setting up operations in Milwaukee and Racine, Wisconsin, and Minneapolis, Minnesota. The Miami-based Untouchables, also known as the Miami Boys, are now pushing crack into Atlanta and Savannah, Georgia, and other cities in the Southeast. Los Angeles gangs have spread to Denver, Colorado, and Vancouver, Washington. According to the *New York Times*, the Bloods and the Crips have also extended their operations to Baltimore, staking claims along the way in middle-size cities like Omaha, and creating distribution networks wherever the market for cocaine and crack looks profitable.

### The Danger of Gangs
Big-city gangs have two advantages over smaller groups and individuals trying to corner the local drug market: they usually

buy directly from top-level smugglers, eliminating the middle-men and getting the drugs wholesale, and they can intimidate local distributors and pushers. Atlanta, Georgia, police lieutenant John Woodward told *Newsweek* that the Miami Boys invaded his city with the attitude that " 'We're *bad* and we'll prove it to you.' [They'll] walk up to [their] competitors and just kill 'em. It's not, 'I'm going to out-macho you.' It's 'I'm going to kill you.' " As the Miami Boys elbowed their way into Atlanta drug distributing, at least thirteen people were murdered in one year. At the same time, in New York City, Chinese criminal "triads" or secret societies have wrested part of the heroin distribution business from the Mafia, while in the city's Chinatown, a Vietnamese gang called "Born To Kill" (BTK) is fighting to take over the illegal businesses the Chinese gangs have replaced with drug trafficking.

While the Mafia and the Los Angeles Bloods and Crips may seem fearsome, experts are equally worried about the emergence and rise to power of the Jamaican gangs. These gangs are called "posses" after the armed bands that chased criminals in American westerns. Most posses were originally marijuana-smuggling rings in Jamaica, and many of their members are illegal aliens. Posses have been growing in Miami, Washington, D.C., and New York, making them a major factor in the crack trade on the East Coast. They are notorious for their viciousness. According to *Newsweek*, posses have been linked to 800 murders, 350 of them in 1988 alone. They prefer to commit their executions on public streets, in restaurants, and in reggae clubs in major cities. Torture and maiming are also posse "trademarks."

As gangs continue to organize and spread, developing for themselves an efficient illegal drug distribution network and a greater stranglehold on the drug business, many experts equate their progress with the growth of the Mafia during Prohibition seventy years ago. The greatest difference, however, is that today's gangs are using military and paramilitary weapons, fighting guerrilla wars in American cities that are far more violent than anything the Mafia ever dreamed of. Using Uzis, AK-47 assault rifles, and AR-15 semiautomatics, gangs today are well prepared to defend themselves against competing groups, enforcement agents, and even U.S. military personnel. Thomas Reppetto, president of the Citizen's Crime Commission of New York told *Newsweek* that "once we let these guys get too big, we've got a situation that will take decades to [control]."

### Fighting the Drug Gangs
Police officers dealing with gangs routinely wear armored vests, even though sometimes the vests do not stop assault-rifle rounds. In addition, many departments give all their officers automatic pistols to increase their firepower. Some cities have trained special task forces to deal with specific gangs. Boston, for example, uses a "Jamaican entry squad" when police must attack a posse stronghold.

Last year in Los Angeles, the police and sheriff's departments swept the south-central section of the city, making more than 12,000 gang-related arrests and thousands more street rousts. The goal was to put Los Angeles's 70,000 gang members on the defensive. New York City is trying a similar effort. Over 100 narcotics agents of the Tactical Narcotics Team target drug-intensive areas of the city such as East Harlem and South Jamaica. The team then floods them one at a time with investigators and undercover officers using "buy and bust" tactics. The arrests they make are almost always of the lowest-level traffickers but the information they gather from confessions can be pooled with the data state and federal agencies need to go after more-important distributors.

In their saturation sweeps, police often use disguises to learn more about drug dealing activities and to catch dealers in the act of making illegal transactions. In Fort Worth, Texas, police posing as trash collectors rode the sanitation trucks to gain the confidence of drug dealers. The ploy led to sixteen arrests. Another rather humorous approach to sweeping areas clean has been dubbed "cop in a box" by Lauderdale Lakes, Florida,

*Young drug dealers in New York City.*
*Gangs are an important part of*
*the drug distribution network*
*in many U.S. cities.*

police. Several police officers hide in an empty carton on the back of a pickup truck while a plainclothes officer drives the truck around looking for dealers. When the driver spots a pusher, he makes a drug "buy." As soon as the money and drugs have changed hands, he toots the truck horn and within seconds the officers have popped out of their box and arrested the dealer.

Saturation tactics are effective in clearing an area of dealers, so much so that when a tactical team decides to move on to another area, the residents of the neighborhoods they are leaving often hate to see them go. They recognize that as soon as the enforcement agents are gone, the dealers will come back. In December 1988 the *New York Times* reported that within two weeks after the Tactical Narcotics Team left southeast Queens, where it had suppressed drug activity for nearly nine months, crack dealers and their addict customers had once again reclaimed the neighborhoods.

A law that could clear some of the worst areas of drug infestation was passed by Congress in 1984. That law expanded the right of the government to seize property involved in drug felonies. Its newest application, however, is the seizure of houses and apartments used for shooting galleries and distribution centers. Once raided, officials then evict the tenants, forcing their operations to shut down, even if only temporarily. This law has become especially useful in public housing projects, where drugs are rampant. Housing Secretary Jack Kemp announced in March 1989 that he had set aside $50 million to rid housing projects of drug dealers by denying dealers leases and evicting those dealers already living there.

Perhaps the most dangerous method police use to learn more about drug traffickers and to build a case against them that will win a conviction in court involves undercover narcotics agents. Posing as a distributor or dealer or as anything from a new kid in school to a hardened criminal in jail, undercover police befriend those who can help them infiltrate the secret circles of dealers and distributors who run the drug trade. By winning the trust of these criminals, agents can begin to trace the flow of drugs back to the most powerful upper-level distributors or gain the information needed to locate drug labs. While all narcotics agents know that they risk their lives fighting drug traffickers, undercover agents place themselves in the greatest danger because they work alone.

## Police Corruption

While murders of law-enforcement agents are becoming more common, the most common technique drug traffickers use to avoid detection is the corruption of citizens and government agents and officials. Drug traffickers use their power and money to buy the allegiance of those who might endanger their operations and those whose aid might increase or simplify their illegal operations. Since 1981, four former sheriffs in Georgia have been convicted for conspiring with drug smugglers. Another sheriff, who refused to resign, is serving time in a federal penitentiary for smuggling marijuana, cocaine, and methaqualone. In both Georgia and Tennessee, men who were "Sheriffs of the Year" in 1980 were convicted in 1984 in separate cases of cocaine trafficking. Another county sheriff was recently charged with taking $50,000 offered by undercover agents posing as traffickers who wanted him to ignore planes flying cocaine into a local airstrip. As with corruption of law enforcement officials in Latin America, money is very persuasive when, according to one member of the President's Task Force on Drugs, ". . . some of these guys are making $14–15,000 a year. And then someone comes along with a suitcase filled with ten years' salary and tells him to just don't do anything. Just go to a movie that night."

In a period of only a few months, police have arrested corrupt agents and officials from every area of the country for all manner of illegal drug-trafficking crimes:

*November 1988.* Three former DEA agents from Los Angeles, for laundering more than $608,000 in money derived from narcotics deals

*December 1988.* Four New Jersey police officers, for distributing cocaine

*December 1988.* Two Orange, New Jersey, police officers, for robbing drug dealers while moonlighting as security guards

*January 1989.* Four U.S. Customs Service employees, for drug trafficking

*March 1989.* Three corrections officers in New York City, for smuggling cocaine to jail inmates

*April 1989.* A counselor at the Spofford Juvenile Center, in the Bronx, New York City, for selling cocaine

In some cases, officers who are themselves addicts are supporting their habits by dealing drugs or taking bribes. New York City wants to minimize the number of officers using drugs by screening applicants, stricter supervision of officers, and random drug testing of all officers, from patrolmen to the commissioner.

For some enforcement officers, especially those in small towns, the influx of flashy cars and big money has tempted them to get in on the action. In a recent *New York Times* interview, Sabastian Garafalo, the mayor of Middletown, Connecticut, said that traffickers use small towns like his to set up laboratories to process drugs. The presence of this illegal activity has fostered corruption among members of his police force, he said.

Oftentimes honest and respected officers or agents get into serious financial debt and succumb to the pressure. In August 1989, the DEA arrested Edward O'Brien, a high-ranking DEA agent. The DEA had carefully planned a sting operation to catch O'Brien and his two brothers, whom they arrested in Boston, Massachusetts's Logan Airport as the brothers arrived from Miami carrying 62 pounds (28 kg) of cocaine. Edward O'Brien had been the head of the Springfield, Massachusetts, DEA office, and was, at the time of his arrest, working out of Washington, D.C., where he had access to top-level information about DEA national and international operations. Allegedly, agent O'Brien had been unable to pay off his loans and was facing foreclosure on his home.

## Money Laundering

While corrupt police are very helpful to illegal drug distributors, they are not as essential as "money launderers," whose services are needed to keep a distributor in business and out of jail. *Laundering* is the processing of illegally obtained, traceable money so that it comes out looking legal, or "clean."

The U.S. Internal Revenue Service requires everyone to pay taxes on his income, even if it's from an illegal source. Of course, traffickers cannot admit to profiting from the drug trade without the risk of being arrested. It is dangerous and difficult for them to get their cash back into the economy in legitimate forms such as loans or investments. It takes money launderers—shrewd accountants, lawyers, bankers, and businessmen—to funnel the money secretly into legitimate businesses so that the traffickers can then claim an honest source of income.

The launderers' schemes often involve the use of foreign banks that keep traffickers' identities secret. Under these circumstances, catching traffickers has required the cooperation of foreign countries. For example, until 1984, the Cayman Islands' banks were a favorite of many drug dealers because of their secrecy laws. In that year an agreement between the Cayman Islands and U.S. governments went into effect that enabled investigators to obtain business and banking records on a case-by-case basis.

Also, U.S. banks are now required to report any transactions they believe involve drug money. The Bank Secrecy Act requires financial institutions to report all transactions of $10,000 or more. The Money Laundering Control Act of 1986 tightened up loopholes and made money laundering even more difficult. An institution that failed to report such transactions could be heavily fined. For example, one California bank incurred a $2.25 million fine by failing to report 7,900 large cash transactions that amounted to $3.98 billion over a five-year period. Another bank in California was fined $4.75 million.

No bank official in either of these cases was charged with

criminal activity. In Texas, however, bank officials were recently arrested for intentional violation of the banking law. The arrest was the work of Operation Cash Crop, carried out by one of the thirteen President's Organized Crime Drug Enforcement Task Forces. Cash Crop discovered that a ring importing marijuana from Mexico was using banks in Texas, California, New York, and the Cayman Islands to launder its profits. When the investigation ended, forty-four people, two companies, and the Texas bank were indicted.

The U.S. government has developed still another way to hurt the wallets of many drug-world kingpins. Until a few years ago, only the money, houses, cars, boats, and planes directly involved in a smuggling operation could be seized when a trafficker was arrested. Though these assets were often worth a great deal, the loss seldom made more than a dent in the traffickers' total assets. The seizures did nothing to permanently disable the traffickers because they often had millions of dollars stashed in foreign banks and laundered in legitimate businesses. "You can put them in jail for ten years and when they get out of jail, if they still have $40 million in bank accounts in Switzerland or Panama or Grand Cayman, they go right back into business," one DEA agent explained. ". . . the only way to put these people out of business is to remove the [money] from the business."

New antinarcotics laws, therefore, have been designed to financially cripple traffickers. The new laws may well be the most effective tactic the government is using. Today any profits that have been made, any laundered money invested in legal businesses, homes, jewels, paintings—anything purchased by drug money—can be seized. From the Texas bank investigation, $6.5 million in drug profits were taken. On the federal level in 1986, enforcement officials' new weapon for squeezing drug traffickers netted them $550 million in cash and property that, according to *Time* magazine, included "race horses, real estate, a surplus Navy bomber, a $25,000 gold-plated motorcycle, high-speed motorboats, a marina, a topless bar, and a pair of Atlanta rib restaurants." In addition, the law passed in 1984 makes it legal to also seize assets that were bought with drug money and subsequently sold or given away. One car, a red 1963 Ferrari racer given to a garage mechanic by a "generous" drug smuggler, recently netted the government $1.6 million.

Alwin Coward, head of financial intelligence for the DEA, told *Forbes* magazine: "We're finding that if you seize every red penny they've got, you render drug trafficking organizations impotent." Operation Pisces caught 387 people, seized $50 million in laundered assets, and froze another $27 million that the Panamanian government had in banks.

Ironically, seized money now pays for the downfall of other drug traffickers because the agency that makes the "bust" often gets to use some of the seized assets for its own operations. Seizures made by the DEA, for example, are turned over to the U.S. Marshals Service until they are forfeited. Then, vehicles and property, sometimes including real estate, can be used by the DEA. Cash goes to participating state and local police and to federal enforcement agencies, based on need. The $500 million seized in February 1989 from Colombian cocaine profits that were being laundered through jewelry merchants from New York to Los Angeles will add a substantial amount of money to enforcement efforts, subsidizing lengthy, dangerous, and always expensive investigations.

### Local Efforts to Fight Drugs
If traffickers believe a profitable market exists in a particular area or if they choose an area for processing or distributing drugs, longtime residents are often helpless to stop them. According to reporter Mark Miller of *Newsweek*, one such town was Martinsburg, West Virginia. Before the drug dealers invaded, Martinsburg's streets were lined with "tidy clapboard houses and neat apple and peach orchards on land George Washington surveyed centuries ago." Many Jamaican migrant workers who usually

came only to harvest fruit took up permanent residence in "the Hill" area, a poor section of town, and "transformed several blocks near the center of town into an open-air drug supermarket." Soon cars were gridlocked at intersections, their passengers lined up to buy from the nearly fifty dealers "hawking dope in broad daylight."

The Martinsburg police were not equipped to handle what happened next. A homicide rate of one or two murders per year leaped to twenty murders, all drug-related, within eighteen months. The drug dealers imported prostitutes to work the streets. In the schools, students caught up in the drug trade "strutted around in expensive Nike jogging suits and gold chains, intimidating classmates and teachers." Needles and knives littered front lawns, and residents lived in fear for their safety.

When, in 1986, Martinsburg asked federal authorities for help, the government sent in 200 agents, who worked with the police to raid drug dens, arrest dealers, and seize their high-powered weapons. Under pressure, the drug trade left, some of it moving 16 miles (26 km) away to Charles Town. But as with all saturation enforcement efforts, once the agents left, the traffickers began sneaking back into Martinsburg. Some residents believe it's just a matter of time before the whole cycle begins again.

Martinsburg is a small town; its population is only 13,000. Yet in the cities, the pattern is the same. *Newsweek* described a drug dealing area of Detroit as a series of "wrecks of burned-out houses, boarded-up houses, vacant lots where houses used to stand. . . . The dealers fortify their houses against rivals, dissatisfied customers and the police, so raids often leave the place a shambles, forcing the operation to move on, like slash-and-burn planters." Drugs were a factor in 38 percent of all murders in a recent year in New York City, up from 20 percent in previous years. Similarly, in December 1988, Hartford, Connecticut, police reported that the drug trade there had increased violence in several sections of the city, leaving nine dead in only three weeks.

Several factors enable drug traffickers to establish their trade in otherwise decent neighborhoods. Sometimes, according to U.S. News and World Report, gangs first gain acceptance by paying their neighbors' rent. If they are setting up operations in a poor neighborhood, this tactic is especially helpful. More often, however, they impose "a reign of terror" on their neighbors, making people afraid to complain. Even when residents do call the police, enforcement agents can do little to stop the traffickers. Simply arresting dealers is not a permanent answer. Traffickers often operate out of "legitimate" businesses such as grocery stores, restaurants, and laundromats. City and federal laws require evidence, arrest, and conviction before the businesses can be seized. Because drug dealers are protected by the same laws as honest citizens, the seizure process often takes months to accomplish.

### Self-Help Efforts

In the meantime, drug abusers invade the area and drug dealers continue to sell their wares. The crime that always accompanies drug trafficking also increases, and honest residents grow frustrated with the government's inaction. "If the system fails," Hubert Williams, president of the Newark, New Jersey, Police Foundation told U.S. News and World Report, "self-help is the ultimate response." Angered by the seeming ineffectiveness of law enforcement agencies, residents often feel they must resort to self-help. But taking a stand against the drug trade is sometimes as dangerous as trying to enforce the laws against it.

In January 1989, for example, when a South Jamaica, New York, resident complained about local drug dealers, his house was fire-bombed. Six people died in the fire that ensued after a similar fire-bombing in Kansas City, Missouri, in February 1989. A Miami grocer, Lee Arthur Lawrence, fought a five-year battle against drug dealers in his neighborhood. The traffickers made many threats against his life, but police could not protect him. He was murdered in March 1989. In August 1989, Brooklyn, New York, residents were outraged when unknown gunmen fired five shots into the home of antinarcotics crusaders Carlos and Maria Hernandez. Mrs. Hernandez died in the attack. The couple had been strong leaders in attempts to rid their neighborhood of drug traffickers.

Despite the danger of retaliation, the residents of many drug-infested neighborhoods still organize to fight back. In Atlanta, a shopping plaza rife with drug dealers led several men to camp out on a drug corner and run an antidrug rally the following afternoon. According to *Newsweek,* one of the dealers forced from his usual place of business told the men, "I could blow you away right here." Although no reprisals occurred in the Atlanta incident, in Compton, California, when a minister organized several antidrug marches, he found the "bloody head of a dog on his desk and a note warning him to stop his crusade or expect the same fate."

While this kind of intimidation is frightening, those most deeply affected by the drug trade fight back because not doing anything is even more frightening. "If people keep running into their houses too afraid to say anything to police, the drug gangs are going to take over the streets," Bill Hopkins, of the New York State Substance Abuse Services, told *Newsweek.* That is why residents of the Ocean View section of San Francisco angrily marched through their streets protesting the drug-related shootings in which two were killed and ten others injured.

Some neighborhoods have adopted harassment tactics in their antidrug campaigns. The East Villagers Against Crack (EVAC) in New York City tried its own form of intimidation by warning dealers in 6-inch (15-cm) painted letters, "You Buy We Spy" and "Drug Dealers Out." EVAC sent letters to everyone in the neighborhood asking them to help fight drugs and formed street patrols. In Glen Cove, New York, grandmothers have organized to patrol the Dan Daly housing project. Their only

*An anti-crack demonstration. Many communities have taken the drug war into their own hands by organizing "self-help" campaigns.*

weapon is their knowledge of the residents. When they see a person they've known all their lives selling drugs, they embarrass or shame him or her.

An interesting by-product of the drug trafficking crisis in the United States is that the relationship between the police and many formerly antagonistic citizens is changing. Where once strong feelings against law-enforcement officers were the rule, today people in many drug-laden communities want tougher police protection and tighter surveillance. In addition, many programs involve the cooperation of citizens' groups and the police, leading to a new camaraderie between the two. In Houston, for example, the police encouraged over a thousand volunteers to march on a park that dealers were using to sell drugs. The marchers drove the dealers from the park and made it clear that they supported police efforts to keep it clear.

Yet while the dealers left the park, Houston police have to remain there all the time or the dealers will be back. This is one of the most frustrating aspects of the war on drugs. Traffickers move their operations, and then they wait until the pressure is off so that they can return. Police forces cannot man every street corner. Citizens' groups can't sustain volunteer patrols indefinitely because their members have jobs and families to support. Sooner or later, traffickers recover lost territories, resuming business as usual.

In a few cases, however, areas have stayed free of traffickers. There groups such as the Guardian Angels or the Muslims have helped by patrolling and controlling the drug trade. Both are citizens' groups armed with walkie-talkies and a belligerence for drug traffickers and other criminals. They are most effective when they live in the neighborhood they patrol. In the New York and Washington, D.C., areas, for example, the Muslims knew the streets. Many were formerly hustlers and local toughs who had found in religion a reason to change their life-style. Muslims believe in self-reliance and discipline and foster black pride. Their religion requires strict adherence to morals and ethics. In a section of Brooklyn, New York, where many lived, drug dealing and street crime were rampant. Then the Muslims decided to take back their neighborhood from drug dealers. They planted themselves in the middle of drug transactions and, using their walkie-talkies, called the police. They scared off would-be buyers and helped police flush out crack houses. While crack houses are hard to close and keep closed, houses in areas guarded by the Muslims "have remained closed since the Muslims began their patrols," Captain Tom Baumann, Police Department, told *U.S. News and World Report.* "We've never seen anything like that before." A similar phenomenon has occurred in the Mayfair Mansions section of Washington, D.C., where one resident maintains that "the Muslims have done more in one day than the police in twenty-two years."

Unfortunately, sometimes even the best-intentioned groups get carried away. Just as the posses of the old West took the law into their own hands, often hanging a suspect without giving him a trial, today many angry citizens' groups are exhibiting the same kind of vigilantism in order to suppress and punish drug criminals.

The two men in Detroit, Michigan, who set fire to a crack house in order to force dealers out are a symptom of this new sentiment—anything is all right if it hurts the drug trade. The men admitted setting the fire, yet they were acquitted in October 1988. According to the *New York Times,* the message to government from the jury that acquitted them and the public is: "Take action, or we will."

But property damage is the least worrisome result of citizens' taking the law into their own hands. Violence has also led to murder. For example, East Harlem, New York, residents mobbed and beat to death a drug addict they claimed had grabbed $20 from a woman in a bakery.

Vigilantism, individuals or mobs taking the law into their own hands, is a dangerous and lawless form of retaliation—and obviously a foolhardy one when constructive approaches abound. Groups that cooperate with the law such as Mothers

Against Gangs or Teenagers in Action or the Southside Concerned Black Men have created school and park patrols, telephone hotlines, and community service groups. In Los Angeles, the Community Youth Gang Services has a $2 million budget to reform former gang members, help ghetto families get counseling, and mediate truces between rival gangs. A television station in Washington, D.C., advises listeners to call its hotline number to report cases of drug dealing. The Citizens Committee for New York City awards grants to neighborhoods with antidrug programs requiring money. Across the United States, private groups and individuals are beginning a legal crusade against drugs that experts hope is only the beginning of a united effort to stop drug trafficking.

A nationwide *Newsweek* poll conducted by the Gallup Organization in August 1989 revealed that 50 percent of all U.S. citizens now believe that the solution to drug trafficking problems will have to be through action taken on U.S. streets. Another 16 percent believe that both international and national measures are necessary, while only 17 percent think that attacking the problem primarily in foreign nations such as Colombia will bring about a solution. The poll indicated that U.S. citizens recognize that the drug crisis can neither be blamed on other countries nor solved by them, and that direct action will have to be taken on the local level if ever the war on drugs is to be won.

In his speech to the nation in September 1989, President Bush reflected that same belief when he stated that the federal government will more than double its aid to state and local enforcement agencies to help them attack the drug problem. Yet most of these funds will be distributed on a matching basis. That means that state and local governments will have to budget an equal amount of money to combat drugs. For many states, cities, and towns already fighting a 43 percent increase in violent crime in the last ten years and already burdened with high costs for increased police personnel, the president's plan does not help enough.

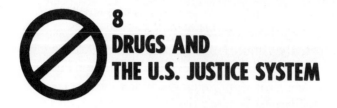

# 8
# DRUGS AND
# THE U.S. JUSTICE SYSTEM

The agencies fighting to dry up the source of drugs—from the DEA all the way down to the most rural police departments—will agree that one of the most difficult barriers to winning the war on drugs is the U.S. justice system. No matter how ominous the drug threat may be, safeguards within the U.S. Constitution and problems with state and federal penal institutions often make combatting drugs more difficult. While that may seem surprising, for three very definite reasons it is not.

1. Congress can arm enforcement agents with laws specifically tailored to paralyze trafficking operations or arrest drug traffickers, but unfortunately, enacting these laws often takes a long time. State and federal legislators have to be educated and convinced before they will support new laws. Many times, the process takes years. When enforcement agents are given the laws to help them cripple traffickers, on the other hand, their job becomes easier. Congress passed the assets seizure law in 1984. After that, those involved in the trafficking of drugs could lose the money, property, and possessions they had accumulated from trafficking profits. After spending a few years in jail, a trafficker could no longer reopen his "business" with the assets

he had illegally accumulated. In addition, the government could use the proceeds from the sale of his properties and the seizure of his bank accounts to pursue other traffickers. The new law made fighting the war on drugs easier for enforcement agencies.

2. The court system, from the U.S. Supreme Court all the way down to the lowest-level local court, is responsible for insuring the rights of every individual as provided for in the Constitution of the United States. Individuals must be proven guilty *beyond a reasonable doubt*. To do so, local and state prosecutors trying a case against a suspected drug dealer must produce evidence that substantiates the government's claims that the individual has committed a criminal act.

The Constitution and laws passed since it was written, however, limit the kinds of evidence the prosecution can use and insure that the evidence it does use is obtained legally. Suppose, for example, that enforcement agents, acting without a search warrant signed by a judge, enter a trafficker's home and seize two plastic bags of heroin they find hidden in a wall. The law would not allow the agents to introduce the heroin as evidence during the trafficker's trial because they searched his home unlawfully. Without a search warrant, they had no right to enter his home. Even though the heroin the agents found clearly implicates the trafficker as a criminal, it could not be used against him.

Suppose also that the remaining, lawful evidence against the trafficker is much less damaging than the two bags of heroin. Basing its verdict on the weak evidence presented, the jury finds the trafficker not guilty, and he is released to continue his criminal activities.

Losing a case against a heroin trafficker because damaging evidence was illegally seized might seem a perversion of justice. Yet the search and seizure laws are designed to protect the rights of everyone—the many law-abiding people as well as the relatively few criminals—by preventing the police from wrongly using their power. The police cannot detain just anyone on the street to search him; they cannot burst into just anyone's home. They have to prove to a judge that they have "probable cause" for the search. In the long run, search and seizure laws and many others like them protect honest citizens from harassment or wrongful accusation and detention. At the same time, however, the laws often make it difficult for prosecutors to put drug traffickers in jail.

3. All federal and state penitentaries are seriously overcrowded. For every trafficker sentenced, someone in jail in the county or state must have served his or her sentence and be ready to return to society. Yet every day, those being sentenced far outnumber those completing their sentences. Judges are forced to make one of two decisions—to send the trafficker to prison but allow someone already there to leave well before his punishment is over, or to let the newly convicted trafficker go. Neither is a decision a judge wants to make, but there is no choice if there aren't enough jails. Thus, drug pushers are often back on the streets within a few hours of their arrest.

### Extradition
One of the greatest difficulties for drug enforcement agents is the international aspect of trafficking. Many of the most important drug traffickers, such as the members of the Medellin cartel, live in Colombia or other foreign countries. U.S. agents cannot enter a foreign country, arrest one of its citizens, and forcibly bring him back to the United States for trial. For a foreign citizen or even a United States citizen residing in a foreign country to be brought to trial, the government of that foreign country must be willing to extradite, or surrender him to U.S. officials for trial.

Extradition is an extremely cumbersome process. It requires the full cooperation of both countries involved, something that seldom happens. Even when relations between the two countries are good, the percentage of successful extraditions is low. In 1986, the U.S. State Department requested the extradition of four people from Belgium, a European ally. Yet only one person was extradited. The government requested eleven extraditions from Canada, its friendly northern neighbor, yet only four were successful. France, Greece, Guatemala, Italy, Jamaica, Mexico, Peru, the Philippines, Switzerland, Thailand, and Turkey, on the other hand, refused every extradition request.

Unfortunately for those working to arrest drug trafficking ringleaders in the countries where drugs are grown, processed, and exported to the United States, the inability to extradite hinders enforcement. According to one official quoted in the *Palm Beach Post*, "We have identified most of the major drug traffickers in the world. The problem is we can't get them here to prosecute them. Our problem is not a law enforcement problem. It's a foreign policy problem."

Foreign traffickers are so fearful of U.S. courts that they will assassinate honest officials who support their extradition. Most experts agree, for example, that the November 6, 1985, assault by communist M-19 "guerrillas" on the Supreme Court building in Bogotá, Colombia, was largely an effort to stop extradition proceedings against several traffickers. Eleven judges were among the ninety-five people killed during that siege, which ended only when the Colombian army stormed the doors. For a time, then, the Colombian government halted extradition proceedings. When, in 1989, President Barcos reinstituted extradition, the retaliatory bombings and assassinations also resumed.

To increase the success of extradition requests, ex-president Reagan began a new foreign aid policy. Each year, those nations receiving foreign aid are reviewed to determine whether they are actively fighting drug trafficking. If a particular nation is not cooperating, it can lose millions of the dollars it needs for domestic programs. The presidential review considers many antitrafficking programs such as crop eradication, destruction of drug labs, and arrests of traffickers, but it also weighs a nation's cooperativeness in bringing known drug traffickers to court in the United States.

### Arresting U.S. Traffickers

While efforts to streamline extradition with foreign countries continue, some officials believe that the DEA should mount a "decapitation" program in the U.S. The program could "cut off the heads" of domestic drug-trafficking operations by targeting the "sales managers" who import and distribute illegal drugs in the U.S. To accomplish this strategy, the DEA would have to nearly double in size at a cost of over $1 billion in the next five years. With 5,500 agents, much more surveillance of suspected ringleaders could lead to far more important arrests.

If the police do mount an intensive campaign against major traffickers, they may have a bloody fight on their hands. As in Latin America, drug kingpins will not easily give themselves up or allow their operations to be destroyed. What is worse, drug traffickers are as well armed as the police. They have at their disposal the drug profits to buy the most sophisticated semiautomatic assault rifles. Strangely, U.S. law allows them to do so. The right to "bear arms" is protected in the Constitution. Although many people believe that the law should be changed, the National Rifle Association has doggedly but successfully fought any form of gun control for decades. Yet today, police argue that something must be done to keep these most devastating weapons out of the hands of traffickers. According to the *New York Times*, imports of semiautomatics by March 1989 had already tripled the amount imported in 1988. California has since banned assault rifle sales, yet President Bush remains opposed to a federal ban.

A proposal meant to please both sides of the gun debate has yet to attain acceptance. It would require a mandatory waiting

*An array of weapons seized from Los Angeles drug gangs. The drug war has created pressure for the banning of semiautomatic weapons.*

period between the order for a weapon and its purchase, during which enforcement agencies could conduct a background check of the purchaser. Joe Casey, the president of the International Association of Chiefs of Police, believes the waiting period also might be a deterrent to drug traffickers.

### Arresting Drug Users

Drug pushers are frequently drug users supporting their habits. Users who sell drugs often pressure other people to try them. In addition, as Congressman Edwards of Oklahoma told the *Washington Post*, "Drug users are the ones who finance the drug trade. They provide the money to operate the drug rings and buy the guns that murder DEA agents. But if they are caught with a small amount, nothing happens." The Anti–Drug Abuse Act, passed in 1986, included a mandatory minimum fine of $1,000 for first-time possession of even a trace amount of an illegal drug and jail sentences for second-time offenses. The law also allowed the seizure and forfeiture of any conveyance carrying drugs, no matter how small the amount.

Using this law as a weapon, near the end of the Reagan administration in 1988, Attorney General Edwin Meese urged federal prosecutors to mount a campaign called "Zero Tolerance." Through Zero Tolerance, the government hoped to shock the public into recognizing that using drugs was a crime that the government intended to punish, and that the punishment for conveying drugs in cars, boats, and private planes, even limited amounts of drugs for personal use, would be costly. The Anti–Drug Abuse law and the Zero Tolerance campaign attack both the demand and supply sides of the drug problem. Their goal is to deter drug use by putting the pressure on addicts and casual users of illegal drugs and also to curb the transfer of drugs from one casual user to another. Within just two months, 1,647 cars that belonged to pushers and drug abusers, with a total value of $25.2 million, were confiscated.

## Testing for Drugs

Other strategies aimed at the demand side of the drug war are also increasing the effectiveness of the supply-side effort. In recent years, as lawmakers have realized that catching everyone holding drugs is not only impossible, but impractical, the federal government has taken a new approach to identifying drug users. While possession of drugs has always been illegal, being under the influence of drugs has not. Yet being under the influence is as much an indicator of recent possession as having the actual drug in hand. If people are tested for the presence of drugs in their bodies, drug users and in many cases drug pushers can be identified. Getting all of them out of the workplace can help stop the flow of drugs into it. At the very least, the risk of being caught using drugs might discourage potential abusers from taking drugs, especially if they know they can lose their jobs. As a result, drug testing has become an important new tool in the war on drugs.

One of the leaders in using drug tests for employees is the federal government itself. In 1986, the federal government decided to set the standard for freedom from chemicals by testing its own employees for drug use. In announcing his new policy, president Reagan said, "The use of illegal drugs, on or off duty, by federal employees is inconsistent not only with the law-abiding behavior expected of all citizens, but also with the special trust placed in such employees as servants of the public." President Reagan issued the new policy in an executive order, which does not require the approval of Congress. The order stated that each agency of the government had to publish a policy regarding drug use and the penalties for offenders. Each agency was also ordered to develop assistance programs for education, counseling, and referral of users for rehabilitation. Finally, all agencies were ordered to begin identifying illegal drug users in "sensitive positions" by testing employees on a controlled and carefully monitored basis. "Sensitive positions" were defined as those in the CIA or the Defense Department or positions in which the employee had access to classified or secret information.

The president's executive order immediately drew criticism from those who view forced drug testing as an invasion of an American citizen's right to privacy. In his article "Reefer Madness," which appeared in *The Nation* shortly before his death, Abbie Hoffman said that "Like the Red Menace of the early 1950s, the current drug hysteria has led to a loyalty oath—this time, the urine test." Another article, which appeared in *Dollars and Sense* magazine, suggested that "Drug tests introduce a new level of surveillance without much promise of eliminating drug use." The president, however, justified his order as a means of preserving national security. He said that those who take drugs evidence "less than the complete reliability, stability, and good judgment that is consistent with access to sensitive information . . . [and] may pose a serious risk to national security, the public safety, and the effective enforcement of the law." Private industry has also begun drug testing. One-fourth of the Fortune 500 companies—IBM, the New York Times, Greyhound, Sunkist, and Union Oil of California among them—now test applicants for illegal drug use.

### The New Drug Bill

While drug testing became the hallmark of the Reagan administration, the Bush administration is pushing a new anticrime bill that has yet to be fully enacted. The *Washington Post* reported in September 1988 that the new bill "would bring sweeping changes to the country's criminal justice system." By substantial margins the House of Representatives added several new amendments to the proposed bill. One would authorize the attorney general to impose a civil fine of up to $10,000 for those caught possessing small amounts of illegal drugs, "even if the individuals are not convicted." The fine could be imposed if "clear and convincing evidence of possession" existed, rather than the evidence "beyond a reasonable doubt" required in a court of law.

One of the most hotly debated amendments to the bill is the "good faith" exemption. If the drug bill passes, this amendment will allow the introduction of evidence that would otherwise have been forbidden by the Fourth Amendment to the Constitution, the amendment that requires a search warrant. The exemption would allow evidence gathered in searches without warrants if the police were acting in "an objective, reasonable, good faith belief" that the search was constitutional. This alteration of a constitutional protection has worried some experts. Scott Wallace, legislative director of the National Association of Criminal Defense Lawyers told the *Post* that the effect of the amendment would be "that virtually no police officer would bother to get a warrant. He'd just have to prove to his own satisfaction that he had a reasonable belief there was probable cause." Others believe that search and seizure decisions against the police have been "wrongheaded", that the Constitution did not intend to forbid the prosecution from using clear evidence in a court of law. They believe that the Fourth Amendment is being used wrongly to punish the police and protect drug traffickers.

The Bush administration wants states to attack the drug trade on the street level by going after drug pushers with every means at their disposal. In his speech to the nation, the president warned drug dealers: "We've all heard stories about drug dealers who are caught and arrested, again and again, but never punished. Well, here the rules have changed. If you sell drugs, you will be caught. And when you're caught, you will be prosecuted. And if you're convicted, you will do time. Caught. Prosecuted. Punished." To ensure that they are punished, the president has proposed "enlarging the criminal justice system across the board, at the local, state, and federal level alike . . . more prisons, more jails, more courts, more prosecutors."

### "Shock Camps" and Other Tactics

"Drug use is wrong . . . and that means the strategy is aimed at reducing drug use," William Bennett, the president's drug-policy adviser, told the *New York Times*. Part of the Bush/ Bennett strategy is the funding of facilities called work camps or shock camps, where convicted drug users will live a spartan, work-oriented, highly structured military-style life until their sentences are completed.

While the new drug bill may be tough on traffickers, many people believe that U.S. "hysteria" over the rise in drug abuse and the power of drug traffickers is dangerous. For example, politicians wishing to respond to the drug crisis are sometimes willing to pass laws that they know are illegal. "It's appalling some of the things we are doing," Congressman Steny H. Hoyer of Maryland told the *Post*. "You have members—good, solid members—come through the door and say, 'I don't care if it's constitutional; we can leave constitutionality up to the courts.' " Others are afraid to stand up against dangerous proposals for fear their constituents will think they're weak on drugs.

Across the nation, legislatures, courts, and law enforcement agents have felt the public pressure to take action against drugs. Today, the right of society to be protected from pushers and drug abusers seems to be taking precedence over the protection of individual liberties. According to the *New York Times*:

- The Delaware state senate seriously considered public whipping as a possible punishment for drug pushing.
- The District of Columbia hopes to expand its new anti-loitering law, which allows authorities to cordon off streets, order people out of an area, and arrest anyone who gathers in groups of two or more people.
- Curfews and street sweeps are becoming common in states such as Florida and Ohio.
- Lawrence, Massachusetts, police have been confiscating the Medicaid and food stamp identification cards of those arrested but not yet convicted on drug charges.
- Berkeley, California, and Alexandria, Virginia, authorities are trying to cut federal rent subsidies and evict the tenants

of homes where police have found evidence of drug dealing, whether or not the tenant was actually involved.

- In Chicago, Operation Clean Sweep seals off public housing projects, conducts house inspections, and requires tenants to produce identification before they can enter the project.
- In Volusia County, Florida, the sheriff stops and searches without a warrant any cars whose drivers fit his drug courier profile. If large amounts of cash are discovered, the money is confiscated as possible evidence of drug trafficking.
- A new California antiterrorism law has made it illegal to be a member of a gang. In Los Angeles, where the problem of street gangs is particularly bad, the district attorney has said he will also seek harsher punishments in criminal cases involving gang members.

While it is clear that these new tactics and laws are designed to help enforcement agents arrest drug traffickers and put them behind bars, they may be undermining United States citizens' civil liberties. The right to freely associate and gather in groups, the right to privacy, and the right to be considered innocent until proven guilty were hard won by the founders of the United States. As Supreme Court justice Thurgood Marshall wrote: "Precisely because the need for action against the drug scourge is manifest, the need for vigilance against unconstitutional excess is great. History teaches that grave threats to liberty often come in times of urgency, when constitutional rights seem too extravagant to endure."

### The Courts' Response
Throughout America, the courts are literally swamped with cases to try, primarily because of illegal drugs. The public's outrage with dealers selling drugs to children on their way to or from school, for example, led to a 1986 federal law that provided

stiffer penalties for drug trafficking within 1,000 feet (about 300 m) of a public or private school. When police in New Jersey cracked down on school pushers, arresting 6,500 of them in 1988, the New Jersey court system had to handle the additional cases. Every time lawmakers write a new law and every time the police mount an intensive campaign against traffickers, the same thing happens. More people are arrested, more must go to trial. If the judicial system is already overburdened, and all experts agree that it is, then the rights of the individual and/or the rights of the public to be protected from criminals must suffer.

That is exactly what is happening. Drug dealers know that they can be arrested several times before they will go to jail. Judges can't send traffickers to jail if the jails have no space, so they put them on what the state of New York calls "interim supervision." This means that the trafficker is free but must regularly report to a state probation officer. The probation officer is supposed to supervise his activities and to ensure that he stays within the law. State probation officers, however, are already overburdened, and the state does not have enough of them to monitor traffickers. "Interim supervision" becomes nothing more than letting the trafficker go.

Another unfortunate by-product of overburdened courts is the increase in plea bargaining—confessing to a lesser charge— to get little or no punishment. Rather than waste the court's time and the taxpayers' money, prosecutors who thought their case against a criminal was a bit shaky often used plea bargaining to insure that he or she received some punishment rather than none at all. The accused person often accepted the plea bargain and pleaded guilty to a lesser crime because he did not want to take the chance of being convicted of the more serious offense. Plea bargaining was a useful tool to shorten court dockets. In recent years with the advent of widespread drug dealing, however, plea bargaining has been used even when the evidence against a trafficker is strong, merely to cope with crowded court schedules and jails with no empty cells.

Another reality of drug crimes and punishments is that although the average sentence for a federal drug offense is about 20 percent longer than it was in 1980, most prison terms are cut short to make room for incoming violators. Thus the justice system becomes a "revolving door," continuously admitting and ejecting drug traffickers, having little effect on the traffickers and providing the public with little protection from them.

### New Penalties

To protect the public and law enforcement officers from the most violent drug traffickers, Congress has included in its new drug bill a mandatory death sentence as punishment for those convicted of drug-related murders. According to the bill, judges would impose the death penalty if a murderer had been involved in at least two continuing criminal operations involving drugs or if the victim was a police officer. If the bill is passed into law, the United States will join twenty-three other nations that have death penalties for drug trafficking. Some of these nations impose the death penalty for simple possession of an illegal drug. Malaysia, for example, automatically executes anyone caught possessing more than 200 grams (7 ounces) of marijuana, 15 grams (0.5 ounces) of heroin, or 1,000 grams (35 ounces) of opium.

Some lawmakers believe the mandatory death sentence will curb drug-related murders by scaring criminals, but others think it will have little or no effect. The latter group point out that while Malaysia has taken the severest stand on trafficking, its drug addiction rate has continued to increase. Others believe that the death penalty might hinder extradition from countries that do not believe in capital punishment. Most of the over 100 extradition treaties the United States has are with countries that have no death penalty.

Should the drug bill pass, the death penalty will deal with the most violent drug traffickers, but other, less violent traffickers must still be punished. The government is considering several proposals, among them work camps and military prisons for dealers. The drug bill proposes denying such federal benefits as housing assistance, job training benefits, and education loans to repeat offenders and requiring random drug testing of those on probation for drug-related offenses.

Meanwhile, the newly appointed chief of the antidrug war, William Bennett, has targeted Washington, D.C., probably one of the worst drug-crime-ridden cities in the United States, to experiment with stronger antidrug measures. Two of his first three strategies are related to the justice system—to expand court staffs to handle drug trafficking cases and to increase jail space. It is clear that those in charge of fighting the war on drugs are disturbed by the government's inability to cope with criminals once they have been arrested, especially when it is spending billions of dollars for the officers and equipment necessary to arrest them.

### Legalization of Drugs

Some people are so disturbed that they have begun advocating the legalization of drugs such as marijuana, cocaine, and heroin. *Editorial Research Reports* quoted University of Southern California law professor Stephen J. Morse: "Despite stunning successes by law enforcement and the criminal justice system that have produced too many drug defendants to try and too many convicted drug criminals to imprison, more dangerous drugs are available at ever-cheaper prices. . . . After about seventy years of unsuccessful federal warring on drugs, let us admit that law enforcement cannot win. . . ."

Morse's opinion is seconded by others who believe that the drug war is unwinnable. They say that Americans do not consider drugs the enemy, at least the millions who use drugs don't. They say that making drugs illegal only serves to produce the crime, corruption, disease, and addiction that the law is trying to prevent. Professor Ethan A. Nadelmann, a Princeton University professor, argues that drug pushers have already won the war, that it would be wiser to face facts and to admit defeat.

"Frankly," said Nadelmann, "I think legalization is a very bad idea. But I also think it's the best of all the available possibilities."

The legalization argument has three parts:

1. *The United States is a free country and people who want to injure themselves should have the right to do so.*

2. *Decriminalizing drugs would destroy their "black market" value and take the profit out of the drug business.* If the drug market were no longer profitable, trafficking organizations would fall apart. If drugs were readily available to anyone, drug bosses, distributors, gangs, and individual dealers would have to find something else to fight about.

Dr. Nadelmann maintains that spending ten times the $8 billion a year the government allocates to drug enforcement probably won't change anything. "It's the old law of supply and demand," Nadelmann told the *St. Petersburg Times*. "As long as the financial incentives are there, there will always be producers and distributors. There's also what's known as a 'push-down, pop-up' factor—push [drug trafficking] down in one place and it pops up in another. . . . You close down one crack house and twenty more open up somewhere else."

3. *The billions of dollars now earmarked for enforcement could be used for the education and rehabilitation of addicts.* Those in favor of legalization maintain that public health would improve after legalization because drug-related violence would decrease and more money would be available for effective prevention of drug experimentation and abuse.

Other experts, however, question just how beneficial legalization could be. They ask difficult questions.

- Should drugs be made available at the corner convenience store?
- Would keeping them out of the hands of teenagers be as unsuccessful as keeping cigarettes from young people has been?

- Would legalization increase experimentation?
- Is the addictiveness of alcohol or cigarettes in any way as intense or dangerous as the addictiveness of heroin? Cocaine? Crack?
- In the long run, does legalization solve anything?

The British tried legalizing heroin, and the United States tried methadone maintenance for heroin addicts, yet the black market for illegal heroin continues in both countries. The Netherlands legalized intravenous heroin use, yet by 1980, its crime rate had continued to rise. When the government tried supplying drugs at centers, junkies from all over the world flocked there. The experiment did not work.

If drugs are to be legalized, the entire world must agree to do so, and it must be willing to pay the price—a price which most people believe is just too high. U.S. citizens would have to be willing to live with the consequences of legalization. According to *Newsweek*, experts predict that decriminalizing drugs would, over time, result in an increase in addiction—as many as 20 million addicts—so that the number of drug addicts would probably equal the number of those addicted to alcohol. The cost of treating so many drug addicts would be astronomical. To rehabilitate all of the 2 million addicts living in the U.S. today would cost between $8 billion and $30 billion a year. Budgeting ten times that amount of money to treat 20 million narcotics addicts would require cutting important defense, educational, or social programs or facing bankruptcy.

The American public, meanwhile, grows more concerned about the drug problem. Because of their growing frustration with the apparent inadequacies of the law and the criminal justice system, many citizens are now willing to try anything, no matter how harsh, to get addicts and pushers off the streets. The courts own the final responsibility for testing a law's constitutionality and protecting individual freedom, but they can be—and in fact have been—influenced by the public's strong, get-tough sentiments against drug trafficking.

In April 1989, for example, the U.S. Supreme Court ruled that police have the right to stop for questioning any airline passengers that fit the DEA "profile" of drug couriers. One danger of this would be that the law and the courts, short-staffed, overwhelmed, and responding to public pressure, may begin to lose sight of the importance of civil liberties. The American justice system faces perhaps the most difficult time in its 200-year history.

# 9
# THE
# NEXT STEP

Near the end of his administration, President Ronald Reagan claimed that the government's war on drugs was "an untold American success story" and that drugs had "already gone out of style in the United States." The president may have had a good reason to make this statement, for the most recent statistics on drug abuse indicated that casual use of drugs had dropped a promising 37 percent. But while casual use has diminished, according to William Bennett, President George Bush's appointed leader in the war on drugs, crack-cocaine addiction is quite another story. "America is now fighting two drug wars, not just one. The first and easiest is against [the] casual use of drugs by many Americans, and we are winning it. The other, much more difficult war is against addiction to cocaine. On this second front," Bennett maintains, "we are losing—badly."

President Bush, who must lead the war on drugs into the 1990s, has had experience with the drug war. It was his job as President Reagan's vice-president to oversee antinarcotics efforts and to coordinate U.S. narcotics enforcement programs. He already knows the difficulties in mounting a war effort against so many and diverse factions, and he has seen effective and ineffective antinarcotics agencies and programs in action.

*President Bush displays a bag of
crack seized by DEA agents
just a few days before in Lafayette Park,
across the street from the White House.*

President Bush is well aware that the national crisis drug abuse has created will not disappear. In fact, it will continue to intensify, and with it, related problems such as AIDS, prostitution, and crime. The state of Connecticut, for example, announced in August 1989 that it had experienced an average 37 percent increase in drug-related crimes across the state and a 100 percent increase in its largest cities. Nationally, the average is 43 percent. The problems drugs create cannot be allowed to continue unabated.

The president has vowed to continue fighting the war on drugs. Yet if he continues with the strategies of the past he will guarantee that his administration will get no closer to winning the war than his predecessor's did. Despite what President Reagan said about his administration's successes, the government's own statistics don't lie. More drugs are coming into the country. More illegal drugs are being grown or chemically produced in the United States. More money is being made from illegal drug sales. Corruption of officials and agents grows more widespread. More people's lives are being jeopardized by drug abuse, and more innocent people are being victimized by drug-related violence and corruption. Finally, those who traffic in illegal drugs are more powerful and wield a greater influence on national and international politics. If the Bush administration hopes to make strides in winning the war on drugs, it will have to come up with something new.

Curtailing the supply of drugs might be possible if the flow of drugs can be disrupted. Experts agree that the Bush administration could significantly disrupt the flow of drugs if it is willing to commit itself to fighting the drug war. Past administrations really have not done so. According to Richard Gregorie, a prosecutor of many federal narcotics cases, historically the drug war has not been a national priority. "I know it hasn't [been]," he said on the *MacNeil-Lehrer NewsHour.*

If you look back over the past eight years, if you find more than one speech by the secretary of state on the narcotics problem, I'd be shocked. I'd also be amazed if you found in our intelligence agencies any kind of priority for dope traffic. In fact, I've talked to a number of State Department people who . . . have said . . . that if you want to reach the end of a career in the State Department, the best way to do it is to get into the narcotics section.

Gregorie's beliefs are seconded by New York congressman Charles Rangel, the chairman of the House Select Committee on Narcotics Abuse and Control. He told *Atlantic*, "We have never fought the war on drugs like we have fought other legitimate wars—with all the forces at our command. . . . This is a war that we have not even begun to fight."

Many people believe that in the past the U.S. government has failed to support the war on drugs because it has other national priorities. They believe that the government has sacrificed major international drug busts and the opportunity to arrest important drug traffickers for political reasons that have nothing to do with drugs. In several recently publicized instances, the government has ignored corrupt leaders who are profiting from the drug trade because the country they represent is strategically important.

For example, for some time the United States has been involved in the political turmoil in the Central American country of Nicaragua. It supported a group of rebels called the Contras, who were fighting to overthrow the Nicaraguan government, run by the Sandinistas. When the Reagan administration believed that Panama's corrupt leader, General Manuel Noriega, could be an ally against the Sandinistas, providing the United States with sites for spying and installations for training Contra guerrillas, it ignored Noriega's involvement with drugs.

"You can't say that the Reagan administration ignored narcotics abroad, but in Central America it turned its head because of [its] obsession with Nicaragua," Francis McNeil, U.S. ambassador to Costa Rica, told the *Palm Beach Post*.

Because the U.S. wanted Noriega's help, it allowed Panama to launder drug money and protect drug shipments. "The foreign policy issue of this country is not narcotics," a high-ranking DEA official told the *Post*. "National security, economics and world trade are."

If the Bush administration puts fighting the war on drugs at the top of its list of priorities, it will pressure drug-trafficking countries to attack the illegal drug industry, and will support the countries that do so. Friendly relations with a foreign country should be based on the country's willingness to extradite drug traffickers for trial in the United States and to destroy drug processing laboratories. While cutting foreign aid can induce some countries to attack traffickers, trade sanctions forbidding imports of produce and products from drug-trafficking nations might also prove to be effective tools for pressure. In addition, as Congressman Rangel said in *Omni* magazine, "Drugs must be depoliticized. Attitudes stemming from the Cold War and four decades of confrontation and preoccupation with communism have diverted attention from drugs, which claim more lives than any conspiracy hatched in Moscow."

Even if the United States government makes the drug war its priority, however, the many agencies with responsibilities over drugs will have to decide that winning the war on drugs is more important than building agency empires and competing for government dollars. According to several sources cited in *Newsweek*, winning the war on drugs has been anything but the real goal for many of these agencies, and because of their "turf wars," the drug-war effort has been sacrificed.

Because the amount of tax dollars allotted to each antinarcotics agency is often dependent on the agency's success in collaring traffickers or seizing contraband drugs, enforcement agencies have begun competing with each other for drug busts —sometimes even if it means letting a trafficker or drug shipment get away.

*Newsweek* described a situation in the Bahamas in November 1988 that is typical of the problem. U.S. Customs' expensive radar tracking system spotted a suspicious plane flying north. They notified Op Bat, a special unit of the DEA designed to disrupt the drug flow through the Bahamas and the Turks and Caicos Islands. Both agencies sent planes and helicopters to pursue the suspected smuggler. When the pilot made a "drop" of illegal drugs into the sea, "the fighting broke out," *Newsweek* said. "—Not with the smuggler, but among the drug agents. Each law enforcement operation wanted to be the one to make the seizure." Because the two agencies refused to cooperate, the pilot got away and the drugs disappeared, picked up by a small speedboat and safely smuggled into the U.S.

Narcotics agencies have been extremely jealous of their turfs, protecting them even when another agency could more effectively capture a trafficker or a cache of drugs. Twelve miles (19 km) beyond U.S. shores, the Coast Guard is responsible for drug smugglers. U.S. Customs and the Coast Guard have joint jurisdiction within the 12-mile limit. Customs is responsible for borders with Canada and Mexico. The DEA has priority inside the United States.

A Customs helicopter recently asked the DEA's permission to seize a boat in the Bahamas that was carrying 1,000 pounds (450 kg) of cocaine. The DEA, which has precedence in the Bahamas, refused its request, so the helicopter had to hover above the boat for nearly two hours until the DEA arrived. Anything could have gone wrong during that time, yet the DEA "had to" seize the load because Bahamian busts "belong" to them.

Not only will narcotics enforcement agencies have to reassess their goals if the war on drugs is to be won, but their efforts need to be coordinated. While different sources claim that different numbers of agencies are presently fighting drugs or overseeing the war effort, the most conservative guess has been thirty separate agencies, seven cabinet departments, and eighty congressional panels, each with its own philosophy and agenda.

President Bush experienced firsthand the seriousness of

coordination problems when as vice-president he was the National Narcotics Border Interdictions System chief. He agrees that "the effort has been hampered, sometimes severely, by inadequate cooperation and coordination." To bring some semblance of order and unification to antinarcotics efforts, Bush saw to it that the 1988 Drug Act created the new position of "drug czar," whose responsibility is to coordinate the activities of all the agencies, task forces, cabinets, and panels and to develop the means and motivation for all of them to cooperate with each other.

Drug coordinating agencies are not something new to the war effort. In fact, the DEA was organized in the early seventies to accomplish much the same thing—to reduce fragmentation among groups and agencies. In 1984, the government also created the National Drug Policy Board to create a "war strategy," but according to *Newsweek*, that resulted in nothing more than a booklet summarizing "other agencies' strategies."

According to the *National Review*, "a [government] coordinator is defined as someone accountable for the results of bureaucracies over which he/she has no control." Although that definition is cynical, most political experts agree that a coordinator will have a difficult time convincing bickering narcotics enforcement agencies to place themselves second to the good of the drug-war effort.

President Bush chose William J. Bennett to be his drug czar, the man to unify narcotics agencies in the war on drugs. As secretary of education in the Reagan administration, Bennett was responsible for encouraging drug-education programs in the public schools. Well before being offered the new drug coordinator's position, he wrote an article for the *National Review* that summarized what may well be his activist's role as drug czar:

> Politics is like football. The game always adds up to sixty minutes, and in Washington, as at Soldiers' Field, either you are on offense or you are on defense.

There is no middle ground and [unlike football] there
is never a time-out. Either you have the ball and are
moving it against them, or they are moving it against
you. My advice is: Move it against them.

Bennett studied the activities of all of the narcotics enforcement
agencies and used the data he gathered to write the 235-page
policy paper which was the basis for President Bush's televised
speech to the nation in September 1989. The Bush/Bennett
policy does not offer sweeping new strategies nor does it promise
any quick solutions, but it has reshuffled the priorities of programs and increased the budget to fight the war on drugs.
The president proposed spending $7.8 billion dollars in 1990.
Approximately 70 percent of those dollars will be spent on
supply-side tactics:

- $449 *million in foreign aid to cocaine producing nations.*
  The emphasis will be on economic support, intelligence
  gathering, and financial support of the law enforcement
  measures taken by foreign governments. While eradication
  programs will be deemphasized, "decapitation" efforts
  aimed at capturing and extraditing drug bosses to the
  United States and seizing their assets will be a priority. The
  administration is strongly opposed to active U.S. troop
  involvement.
- $1.6 *billion for border control*
- $3.1 *billion to state and local governments* to step up "street
  level" attacks on both traffickers and users
- $1.6 *billion for federal corrections facilities* to house the
  increased numbers of convicted traffickers

Congress responded to President Bush's request by adding $1.2
billion to his budget, an indication of the importance both the
Republican and Democratic parties place on waging a full-scale
war on drugs.

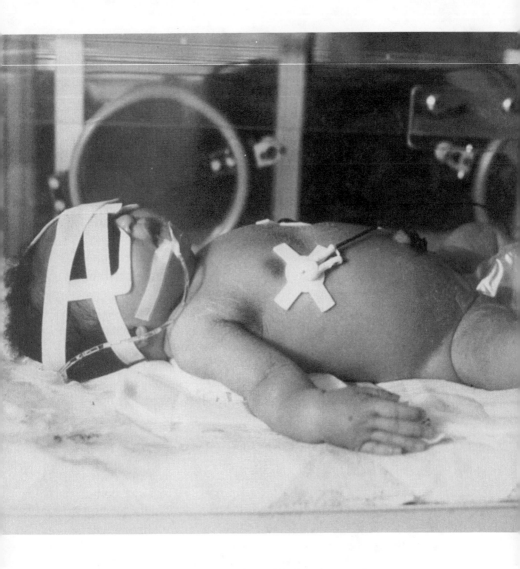

*The addicted baby of a crack user in a neonatal intensive care unit. These littlest victims of drug abuse are truly "lifelong casualties."*

While in his requests the president did not choose to emphasize demand-side efforts, he by no means has ignored their importance. Expanded treatment programs—including removing addicts from their neighborhoods and developing their job skills to prepare them for entering the work force—and pressuring schools, colleges, and universities to institute drug prevention and education programs are also part of the Bush/Bennett strategy.

In addition to committing itself to an all-out effort to fight drugs, to ending turf wars among agencies by appointing a coordinator to unify all antinarcotics efforts, the Bush administration will also have to fund crop incentive plans, which need research to find a way for Latin American farmers to make more money from legal crops than from growing coca. Aerial spraying programs could be increased if the research could develop less harmful herbicides. The technical equipment to detect illegal drug shipments must also keep pace with the increasing sophistication of drug smugglers.

The United States government has much to do to win its war against the power of drug trafficking networks and their addictive contraband. A world in which no addictive drugs exist (except for medical and scientific use) and in which none of the problems drugs create exist will require an all-out and costly effort over the next several years. There are no quick solutions. But while the government can spend billions to fight the war, and while narcotics agents and other police officers can continue to risk and sometimes lose their lives to bring traffickers to justice, it will be the determination of United States citizens that will in the long run win the war.

U.S. citizens have now begun to recognize that the drug crisis affects each and every one of them. They can no longer ignore blatant drug abuse in their neighborhoods. They can no longer allow drug use to be a socially acceptable form of recreation. Adults and young people alike have begun to recognize that relatives, friends, or fellow employees who sell or use drugs are nothing less than public enemies. Sellers and users of illegal drugs support those criminal organizations that have become the most serious threat to the stability of the United States and foreign nations everywhere. Frightened and yet enraged by the viciousness and strength of international drug cartels and domestic traffickers, U.S. citizens realize that only by supporting their government's war on crime will the war be won, as President Bush stated, "—neighborhood by neighborhood, block by block, and child by child."

# BIBLIOGRAPHY

Apple, R. W. "Short of the Mark." *New York Times*, September 7, 1989.

Baasher, Taha. "Preventing Drug Problems." *World Health*, August/September 1985.

Baer, Donald, and Duffy, Brian. "Inside America's Biggest Drug Bust." *U.S. News and World Report*, April 11, 1988.

Begley, Sharon. "The Long Road Back." *Newsweek*, May 11, 1987.

Berg, Paul. "Cocaine's Deceit: Luring the Brain Down the Path of Addiction." *Washington Post*, May 14, 1986.

Berke, Richard L. "New Stress on Old Ideas." *New York Times*, September 6, 1989.

——. "Parties Skirmish About Strategy in War on Drugs." *New York Times*, September 6, 1989.

"The Big Push." *Sierra*. November/December 1988.

"Breakthrough Against Cocaine." *Reader's Digest*, April 1987.

Brooke, James. "Colombia's War." *New York Times*, August 27, 1989.

Bureau of International Narcotics Matters, U.S. State Department. *International Narcotics Control Strategy Report*. March 1, 1988.

Church, George J. "Fighting Back." *Time*, September 11, 1989.

——. "Going Too Far." *Time*, September 4, 1989.

Clare, Anthony W. "Drugs Are Big Business." *World Health*, June 1986.

Comptroller General of the United States. *Controlling Drug Abuse: A Status Report*. General Accounting Office, 1988.

Contreras, Joseph. "Most Wanted in Medellin." *Newsweek*, September 25, 1989.

"Controversy Over Omnibus Drug Legislation." *Congressional Digest*, November 1986.

Cooper, Mary. "The Business of Illicit Drugs." *Editorial Research Reports*, May 20, 1988.

Cooper, Nancy. "Drugs, Money and Death." *Newsweek*, February 15, 1988.

Corn, David, and Morely, Jefferson. "Beltway Bandits." *The Nation*, April 17, 1989.

"Crack: Hour by Hour." *Newsweek*, November 28, 1988.

Cummings, John. "Save the Planet." *Omni*, September 1989.

Davies, Owen. "Addicted!" *Health*, July 1987.

"A DEA Hero Is Busted." *Newsweek*, August 28, 1989.

de Fondaumière, B. Juppin. "International Control of Drugs." *World Health*, June 1986.

Doerner, William R. "Flames of Anger." *Time*, January 18, 1988.

"The Drug Czar: No 'Walter Wallflower.'" *Science*, March 10, 1989.

"Drug Programs Show Mixed Results." *USA Today*, August 1987.

Emmerman, Lynn. "The Dealer and Mr. Clean." *Chicago Tribune*, October 26, 1986.

"Evolution of Current Drug Legislation." *Congressional Digest*, November 1986.

"Federal Agencies Involved in Omnibus Drug Legislation." *Congressional Digest*, November 1986.

"The Federal Express Connection." *Newsweek*, August 21, 1989.

Gentile, William. "A Bungled Deal With Panama." *Newsweek*, April 10, 1989.

"Getting Tough on Cocaine." *Newsweek*, November 28, 1988.

Goodstadt, Michael S. "School-Based Drug Education: What Is Wrong?" *Education Digest*, February 1987.

Gordon, Jeff. "The Cocaine Drain—How St. Louis Teams Are Attacking It." *St. Louis Post-Dispatch*, July 6, 1986.

Gorriti, Gustavo A. "How to Fight the Drug War." *Atlantic*, July 1989.

Graham, Bradley. "The Phony War Against Cocaine." *Washington Post*, July 27, 1987.

Grant, Marcus. "Meeting the Threat of Drug Abuse." *World Health*, June 1986.

Grimm, Fred. "Moonshiners' Network in Dixie Adapts Easily to Cocaine Trading." *Miami Herald*, December 11, 1985.

Hackett, George. "Saying 'No' to Crack Gangs." *Newsweek*, March 28, 1988.

Henkel, Ray. "Going Right to the Source." *Arizona Republic*, July 2, 1986.

Highfield, Roger. "Designer Drugs." *World Health*, June 1986.

"Highlights of the House Bill." *Congressional Digest*, November 1986.

Hoffman, Abbie. "Reefer Madness." *The Nation*, November 21, 1987.

Hunt, Frances A. "Are the National Forests Going to Pot?" *American Forests*, March/April 1987.

"International Narcotics Control Strategy Report." *Department of State Bulletin*, April 1987.

Jalon, Allan. "Deep Inside the Pill Trade." *Los Angeles Times*, June 8, 1986.

Kalix, Peter. "Chewing Khat." *World Health*, June 1986.

Kenworthy, Ken. "House's Tough Antidrug Bill Called War on Bill of Rights." *Washington Post*, September 19, 1988.

Kerr, Bob. "Marijuana: Growing Up in Smoke." *Providence Journal Bulletin*, November 2, 1986.

Khan, Inayat. "Escape into Nightmare." *World Health*, June 1986.

Kline, David. "How to Lose the Coke War." *Atlantic*, May 1987.

Koepp, Stephen. "Sniffing Out a Line of Coke Brokers." *Time*, April 27, 1987.

Kreiter, Marcella S. "Fighting Drugs: A Look at the New Laws and Changed Attitudes." *Current Health*, April 2, 1987.

Lacayo, Richard. "On the Front Lines." *Time*, September 11, 1989.

Lawn, John C. "Drugs in America: Our Problem, Our Solution." *Vital Speeches*, March 15, 1986.

Lee, Rensselaer W., III. "The Latin American Drug Connection." *Foreign Policy*, Winter 1985–86.

Leepson, Marc. "The Fight Against Drug Smuggling." *Editorial Research Reports*, February 8, 1985.

Levine, Art. "Drug Education Gets an F." *U.S. News and World Report*, October 13, 1986.

Lyon, Linda. "Cocaine's Children." *Palm Beach Post*, October 5, 1986.

Marks, Peter. "Busted for Life." *Newsday*, June 7, 1987.

Marriott, Michel. "Doubts Greet Drug Plan in New York." *New York Times*, September 7, 1989.

Martz, Ron. "Drug: Bad News from the Battlefront." *Palm Beach Post*, October 16, 1988.

_____. "For Poor Farmers, Drugs Bring Money by the Bushel." *Palm Beach Post*, October 16, 1988.

_____. "Front Lines Like Vietnam: Few Victories, Vague Plans." *Palm Beach Post*, October 17, 1988.

_____. "Narco-terrorism: New Way to Shoot Up." *Palm Beach Post*, October 19, 1988.

_____. "Opium, Hashish Profits Fuel Lebanon's Holy Wars." *Palm Beach Post*, October 18, 1988.

_____. "U.S. Plays Global Politics as Anti-Drug Efforts Fade." *Palm Beach Post*, October 17, 1988.

McBee, Susanna. "Flood of Drugs: A Losing Battle." *U.S. News and World Report*, March 25, 1985.

Mills, James. "The Underground Empire." *Palm Beach Post*, July 13–14, 1986.

Morganthau, Tom. "Hitting the Drug Lords." *Newsweek*, September 4, 1989.

Morganthau, Tom, et al. "The Drug Gangs." *Newsweek*, March 28, 1988.

Morganthau, Tom, and Miller, Mark. "The Drug Warrior." *Newsweek*, April 10, 1989.

Morganthau, Tom; Miller, Mark; and Contreras, Joseph. "Now It's Bush's War." *Newsweek*, September 18, 1989.

Morganthau, Tom; Miller, Mark; and McDaniel, Ann. "Bennett's Drug War." *Newsweek*, August 21, 1989.

Murphy, Joe. "Seen but Not Heard: Chemically Dependent Abuse Victims." *Arms Acres Newsletter*, Fall 1987.

Musto, David F. *The American Disease: Origins of Narcotic Control*. Oxford University Press, 1987.

Mydans, Seth. "Powerful Arms of Drug War Arousing Concern for Rights." *New York Times*, October 16, 1989.

National Narcotics Intelligence Consumers Committee (NNICC). *The NNICC Report 1987: The Supply of Illicit Drugs to the United States*. April 1988.

"The New Kid." *Time*, November 9, 1987.

"On Noriega, 'We Have Failed Miserably.'" *Newsweek*, September 4, 1989.

Ostling, Richard N. "Filling Uncle Sam's Auction House." *Time*, December 14, 1987.

Ovack, Kathleen. "Cocaine: Unpredictability Makes Using Drug a Deadly Gamble." *St. Petersburg Times*, July 13, 1986.

Phalon, Richard. "Sobering Facts on Rehab." *Forbes*, March 9, 1987.

Pitt, David E. "Panamanian Tells of Goal of Rebels." *New York Times*, October 13, 1989.

"President Reagan's Executive Order." *Congressional Digest*, May 1987.

President's Commission on Organized Crime. *America's Habit: Drug Abuse, Drug Trafficking, and Organized Crime*. March 1986.

Ricks, Thomas. "Cocaine: Now a Part of Corporate U.S." *Miami News*, July 10, 1986.

Robbins, C. A. "America on Drugs." *U.S. News and World Report*, July 28, 1986.

Salholz, Eloise. "Send in the Troops?" *Newsweek*, September 4, 1989.

Satchell, Michael. "Narcotics: Terror's New Ally." *U.S. News and World Report*, May 4, 1987.

Schmalz, Jeffrey. "On Battleground of the Street, Few See a Victory Over Drugs." *New York Times*, September 7, 1989.

*Schools Without Drugs*. U.S. Department of Education, 1986.

Schwarz, Michael. "Deadly Traffic." *New York Times Magazine*, March 22, 1987.

Seligmann, Jean. "Crack: The Road Back." *Newsweek*, June 30, 1986.

Shannon, Elaine. "Desperados." *Time*, November 22, 1988.

"Should Hard Drugs Be Legalized?" *St. Petersburg Times*, June 5, 1988.

Spencer, Jim. "The Drug Warrior: My Job Is to Free America of Addiction." *Chicago Tribune*, October 26, 1986.

Stein, Mark. "Marijuana Crop—An Uneasy Life." *Los Angeles Times*, June 23, 1985.

Treaster, Joseph B. "Colombians Hail Bush's Drug Plan." *New York Times*, September 7, 1989.

"Turf Wars in the Federal Bureaucracy." *Newsweek*, April 10, 1989.

Uehling, Mark. "Drug Rehab: The Addict Glut." *Newsweek*, August 25, 1986.

"Unveiling Bennett's Battle Plan." *Newsweek*, April 24, 1989.

United Nations. "No to Drugs, Yes to Life." *UN Chronicle*, May 1987.

Vera, J. Martinez. "Supplying the 40 Million Who Won't Say No." *World Press Review*, May 1988.

Walsh, Kenneth T.; Taylor, Ronald A.; and Gest, Ted. "The New Drug Vigilantes." *U.S. News and World Report*, May 9, 1988.

Watts, Marianne. "Fighting Cocaine's False Promises. *Dare*, vol. 1, no. 3, 1986.

Weinraub, Bernard. "President Offers Strategy for U.S. on Drug Control." *New York Times*, September 6, 1989.

Weiser, Benjamin. "A Child Living in a Heroin Gallery." *Washington Post*, January 3, 1988.

Whitefield, Mimi. "Drug War Failing, Home and Abroad." *Miami Herald*, December 8, 1985.

"White Lines, Bottom Lines." *Dollars and Sense*, December 1986.

Winstead, Joy. "Druggie Tale Told Easily: Lesson Is Hard." *Richmond Times-Dispatch*, January 13, 1985.

—————. "Intensive Last-Resort Program Helps Drug Abusers Go Straight." *Richmond Times-Dispatch*, January 13, 1985.

X., Richard. "Confessions of An Aging Pothead." *Texas Monthly*, vol. 14, no. 5, May 1986.

Zaldiver, R. A. "Real Enemy in Drug War Is Hard to Define." *Miami Herald*, December 12, 1985.

Zurer, Pamela. "Scientists Struggling to Understand and Treat Cocaine Dependency." *Chemical and Engineering News*, November 21, 1988.

# INDEX